THE GOLDEN, OLDEN DAYS

Growing Up Poor and Not Knowing It

Our Mother and Father—
Ethel Gertrude Kemp and
Fred Joseph Kemp

THE GOLDEN, OLDEN DAYS

Growing Up Poor and Not Knowing It

■

An Autobiographical
Family Biography

by

JAMES MALCOLM KEMP

KEMP PRESS

THE GOLDEN, OLDEN DAYS
Growing Up Poor and Not Knowing It

AN AUTOBIOGRAPHICAL FAMILY BIOGRAPHY

by
JAMES MALCOLM KEMP

Copyright© 1991 by James M. Kemp
Library of Congress Catalogue Card Number 91-93118
ISBN 0-9630899-0-0

First printing

*To purchase copies directly
call or write:*

JAMES M. KEMP
15 Judkins Avenue
Bath, Maine 04530
Telephone: 207 443-4532

Printed and designed by
Fred Weidner & Son Printers, Inc.
New York, New York

Typography by
Robert S. Keefe

*This work
is dedicated to the memory
of my mother,
Ethel Gertrude Kemp,
and my father,
Fred Joseph Kemp.*

*They were two remarkable people
who lived their lives
with quiet, unassuming nobility,
exhibiting an indomitable spirit
as they surmounted all obstacles.*

*Now that I approach
the number of years granted to them
and have experienced life
in most of its dimensions,
I am in awe of what they accomplished.*

*I thank them for the gift of life,
and their examples
of how it should be spent.*

*Truly,
they were worthy of emulation and praise.*

ILLUSTRATIONS

THE GOLDEN, OLDEN DAYS
Growing Up Poor and Not Knowing It

CONTENTS

ACKNOWLEDGMENTS

My wife, Lavina, has been, as always, a constant support, particularly when I wandered too far afield from the story I was trying to unfold. Her gentle comments and asides have kept me in focus.

Pat Dobbins, who typed the numerous drafts of this tome and deciphered my handwritten scrawl, also encouraged me to continue this effort. Without her typing and word-processing skills, this narrative might still be a sheaf of scribbled papers.

Rosemary Bunn and Lucie Teegarden, my "first readers," lent invaluable assistance as I struggled with my old nemeses of punctuation, grammar and spelling.

The illustrations are from old family photographs, and from sketches by the author. Rick Cowley provided the photographic technology required in preparing these for printing. The Wesley Church sketch is used with the permission of Mrs. George H. Kronberg, Office Manager.

PROLOGUE

In many ways, this narrative is about a house and the family that lived in it as well as being recollections of my childhood. They all are inextricably intertwined. It recalls my experiences, thoughts and feelings from earliest memories until the age of fourteen, spanning the years 1926 to 1937.

Some is factual, some is conjecture. Some may be fantasy— things as I would like to remember them. Time has a way of softening or eradicating sad, unhappy, disagreeable memories while strengthening recollections of the happy, pleasant, wondrous, exciting, awesome things which make up our lives. If this were not so, we would be reluctant to recall those events of yesteryear—to relish them as "the best years of our lives."

My memories are my own. My brothers and sisters, while sharing some of my remembrances, will have their own, different from mine. Still, we retain a common core of happy times together.

My sister Phyllis and I sometimes debated whether we were "poor." I am sure our brothers and sisters did the same. Our conclusion was always the same—that we were not. Poor people were on "relief." Their fathers, out of necessity, often worked on W.P.A. projects or sold polished apples on Main Street; some families even lived at the "poor farm." We lived in our own house, did not want for food and clothing, and even had time for music, reading, family fun and many other things that really mattered. It was comforting to come to this conclusion and go to our beds with this sure and certain blessing, and the blissful sleep which followed.

How did this happen: that I am now a "Senior Citizen," a retired gray panther, the father of four middle-aged children, when I still often think and feel like a young man—sometimes even like a child—trapped in an old man's body? Some who read this who are of my vintage, may share these thoughts and memories and also long for those halcyon days when life was simpler and sweeter, when we lived first-hand as active participants rather than as passive recipients or spectators of life.

Our children and grandchildren ask on occasion what life was like in the "olden days": before TV, computers, Xerox, Fax, air conditioning, electric dishwashers and dryers; before jet planes, space probes, men on the moon; before supermarkets, shopping malls, credit cards, plastics, frozen foods, instant soup; freeways, traffic gridlocks, suburban developments, high-rise apartments, condominiums; little league sports, aerobics, jogging and weight-watching clinics; before the holocaust, atomic energy, nuclear arms races, home bomb shelters, acid rain; single parenthood, open marriages, commuter marriages, aid to dependent children; a time when government subsidies were not available to meet every perceived need that we would not or could not provide for ourselves; when victims received more protection under the law than did criminals, and to be gay simply meant to be keenly alive, exuberant and of a merry spirit with no connotation of homosexual behavior; before the spectra of drug and alcohol addiction among children as well as adults, with drug-war reports a common news item; when the fluent use of vulgar, foul, obscene and violent language was not a criterion of sophistication, and conversations could be held without endless strings of jargon words and phrases, non-sequiturs and "sound-bites."

CHAPTER I

The Family

WE WERE A LARGE FAMILY—mother, father, and eleven children (six girls, five boys), whose births spanned twenty-one years. We were all born at home in our parents' bed, the bed which was given to me by "Ma" when she moved from her home of fifty-five years. It has been treasured in my own home for over thirty years.

My Mother and Father *("Ma" and "Pa")*

Ma was born on March 23, 1885, in MacPhee's Corner, Nova Scotia, and was of Scottish heritage by way of her MacPhee ancestors. She was orphaned at the age of four, as were her brother Fred and sisters Eunice and Nettie. These children were by necessity parcelled out to relatives. Ma travelled alone by ship from Halifax to Boston at age nine to live with relatives she had never met—Uncle John Welch, I believe. There she earned her daily bread as a maid or servant in that household. Her formal schooling ended at that time, at a grade five level. At the same time her cousin, Maude, with whom she lived, and who was of the same age, went off to school each day. This must have been a sad and wrenching experience for Ma. She told me that Maude often reviewed the lessons of the day with her. In this way she was able to experience some semblance of a grammar school education.

Pa was born on September 21, 1874, in Kingsley Falls, Quebec, and was of English and Scottish stock. His more immediate ancestors were pre-Revolutionary immigrants to Massachusetts and New Hampshire. His great-great-grandfather, Humphrey Jackman of Bradford, New Hampshire, served in American military regiments during the Revolutionary War. His original gravestone, with the permission of Bradford town officials, is now a table-top in my family room. It had been replaced with a more imposing marker by his son, Samuel Jackman. James Jackman, an even earlier ancestor, was one of the early seventeenth-century settlers of Newbury, Massachusetts. Pa's father, Joseph H. Kemp, was drowned in Kingsley Falls, Quebec, when Pa was only three years of age. Family legend has it that Grandpa Kemp was on duty as a member of the Royal Canadian Mounted Police at the time of his death.

Pa's mother, Salina Jackman Kemp, married George Wilkins following this tragedy. Shortly thereafter they moved the family, including Pa's sisters Allie and Ada and brothers John and Willis, to Worcester, Massachusetts. Pa was also put to work—as a stable boy—when he was nine years old, thus ending his formal education at that time. One of his jobs was to lead the teams of horses pulling the pre-electric trolley cars up the hills of South Main Street. This, I believe, was the source of his life-long love of horses.

The fact that both Ma and Pa were put to work at age nine rather than attending school—in violation of at least today's child labor laws—adds credibility to the conjecture that they both may have been brought into this country as illegal immigrants. It may be that school or immigration officials were simply not aware of their residence here.

It seems that Ma's strong religious convictions were nurtured by Uncle John Welch. He served as a missionary to Boston waterfront seamen, attached to the Beacon Hill Seamen's Chapel. This is also undoubtedly the root of her devotion to the works of The Salvation Army and The Women's Christian Temperance Union, her love of reading, of classical and sacred music, and of all formal learning. It appears likely that she migrated to Worcester in her early teen-age years to serve as a maid in a wealthy household. Through those experiences she gained an appreciation of an elegant way of life. This was reflected in her use of proper table linen, dishes, silver service, crystalware, her practice of proper and genteel speech and manners at table and elsewhere, her belief in the importance of correct dress for every occasion, and in her appreciation of well-kept flower gardens, lawns and other landscaping niceties. These traits, despite our limited financial resources, were transmitted to us, her children, and can still be observed to some degree in our lives today.

By the time Pa was about twenty years of age he had established his own business as a milk dealer, buying milk from farmers of surrounding towns, and distributing it throughout the city of Worcester. I think he must have met Ma in the course of his deliveries to the homes in which she served.

They were married on November 30, 1904, in Trinity Methodist Episcopal Church, Worcester, and immediately moved into their new Victorian-style home located at 552 Chandler Street in the northwestern outskirts of the city. She was always "Gertie" to him; he was always "Fred" to her.

Reflections on Ma and Pa

They rose well before dawn each day to enjoy the splendor of sunrise, the calls of awakening birds, and simply the peace and quiet of those hours. These were the times they read—often to each other—from the Bible and religious commentaries. Several of their volumes are in my library. The one which I prize the most is an 1841 translation of Thomas à Kempis' *The Imitation of Christ.* It is small, well-worn and fragile. My conjecture is that Ma brought it with her from Nova Scotia. Ma had read the complete Bible three times—Old and New Testaments—and was well into her fourth reading at the time of her death. Together, they also made forays into Dickens, Emerson's Essays, the writings of Abraham Lincoln, and other literature of a similar genre. They extended their learning in this way, far beyond the scope of their limited formal schooling.

These were also the hours, before her children awakened, that Ma taught herself to play the piano, using the manuals of her daughters who took formal keyboard instruction. Her many tasks began shortly thereafter—kneading and baking bread, preparing breakfast, washing clothes by hand, ironing, house cleaning. Pa had long departed on his milk delivery route. Pa worked hard during the day as well—cutting firewood, mowing the hayfields of neighboring farms, planting and cultivating vegetable gardens, running his milk processing and bottling plant. In later years when he owned a grocery store, he made his early morning produce purchases at the wholesale farmer's market in Salem Square.

His six-foot, hand-forged crowbar and his bucksaw are two other articles of my legacy. Whenever I use them I am reminded of his powerful, gnarled hands which once grasped these implements as mine now do.

Pa mowed the back fields—beyond the woods and swamp—with a two-horse rig. Ma joined him at lunch-time. They sat on a stone wall in the shade of bordering oak trees, enveloped in the scent of new-mown hay, and feeding crusts of bread to chipmunks who lived in the wall. On one occasion Pa was bitten by one of these little creatures. The blood poisoning which followed required the amputation of his left index finger. (We children were intrigued with this stump of a finger!)

Pa frequently whistled a tune as he went about his work—more often than not Bobby Burns' "Coming Through the Rye." When particularly stumped by a task he might vent his frustration with a quiet "Gorram," "Jiminy Christmas" or "Gee." I never heard him take the Lord's name in vain or use any form of profane language other than these mild slang expressions. Neither he, nor certainly Ma, ever partook of beer, wine or liquor, or any form of tobacco. These were unknown commodities in our home. (Ma's strong convictions concerning the evils of drink were expressed in later years upon my return home on Navy leave during World War II after two years of sea-duty as, "James, a drop of liquor has never passed my lips and I wish I could say the same for you.")

One of Pa's most memorable adventures during his teen-age years was a one-day trip to Amherst with a friend, on high-wheeled bicycles. This was quite an accomplishment since the round trip over hilly, rutted dirt roads was more than eighty miles!

Our family enjoyed a relatively prosperous life during the 1920's. Pa's milk dealership (Maple Grove Dairy—Milk and Cream) flourished by dint of the long, hard hours devoted to it by our parents as well as my older brothers and sisters. This was evidenced by a mortgage-free home, a new four-door Oldsmobile sedan, and the frequent serving of roast beef, steaks and pork chops, along with other signs of prosperity.

My brothers helped Pa on his milk delivery route, completing this chore before their school day began. In some respects these duties were not unlike those of farm boys who were up and out in the barn before dawn feeding the stock and milking cows prior to breakfast and school. I never had this experience since Pa had gone out of the milk business before I was old enough to lend a hand.

The Great Depression following the stock market crash of 1929 had its terrible impact on us as on countless other families. The milk business failed; customers were unable to pay their bills. The house was mortgaged. Two acres of our cornfield were sold as house lots. The barn was torn down by Pa and my brothers to reduce property taxes, and to sell the timbers, planks and boards. Harnesses, horse collars and other equipment for hitching horses were sold for what they might bring. Cheap second-hand cars replaced the Oldsmobile.

Cordwood replaced coal for our furnace and stoves. Trees were cut from the back woods, trimmed, and hauled home by my father and older brothers using axes and two-man cross-cut "hand-powered" saws. The "cellar way," a passage of stone walls under the milk-room, was the marshalling area for logs. One of my fall chores was to buck-saw and split them into stove lengths, storing them in the cellar under the turret.

Come what may, our parents would not even consider seeking welfare, W.P.A. jobs, or other forms of public assistance. Through it all, Ma and Pa continued to enjoy mid-morning and mid-afternoon tea together and to dream of a farm in the country. These hopes were kept alive by rides through country towns to view prospective properties. They never, in all their years together, went on holidays or vacation trips other than annual visits to the beaches of New Hampshire and Maine or to the White Mountains, always accompanied by several of their children. Neither of them ever returned to the Canadian homes of their birth although they expressed a longing to do so. Perhaps they feared they would not be able to leave or re-enter the United States because of the circumstances under which they entered this country as children.

During these years, Pa opened his grocery and produce store, delivering some of his wares to several saloons in the city. He once commented that he could not understand how men could idle away their time in these establishments, drinking schooners of beer to wash down pickled eggs and potato chips. He expressed the hope that I would never frequent these smoke-filled dens. Later, he took a job as groundskeeper for the athletic fields of Worcester Polytechnic Institute. After ten years of these duties, he became the night watchman. Thus, he was able to spend a few hours of daylight on his five-acre farmland in the town of Leicester, raising chickens and truck vegetables, both for home consumption and to sell eggs and produce from our roadside stand. He retired from WPI at about the age of seventy-five. It seems that he had subtracted ten years from his age in order to get the job originally!

I recall vividly the day that Pa returned from his farmland in his 1932 Plymouth. I was mowing the side lawn and was about thirteen years of age at the time. I wondered why he did not immediately alight from his car, but rather just sat there for a time while Ma watched in anticipation from the back porch stairs. Finally the door opened as he extended his axe as a sort of a cane, followed by his left leg which he held out stiffly. When Ma asked him if he was all right, he responded, "I think I hurt my leg a little bit, Gertie." He then asked me to "help him a little." Leaning on my shoulder, he made his painful way to the porch and kitchen. It turned out that a tree had fallen on his leg while he was cutting firewood. It was broken below the knee. He had hoisted himself stoically into the car and driven himself home despite the pain. He wore a full-leg cast for three months or more, but after the first week or so went about his work on crutches as best he could.

Pa died in 1957, in his eighty-third year. Ma passed away, also at age eighty-three, in 1968.

Brothers And Sisters, All

My brothers and sisters were:

JOHN FREDERICK, born in 1905, died in 1924 at age 19. Ma and Pa never fully recovered from this loss of their first-born child. I have no memory of him, being only one and one-half years of age at the time of his death. He is remembered by others for his warm, thoughtful, outgoing personality, his wit and humor, and his love of rugged outdoor recreation. I wore his pale blue, hand-tied bow tie on Sundays as a child.

EVA GERTRUDE, born in 1907, died in 1983 at age 76. She left home at age 16 (in the year of my birth) to earn a baccalaureate degree from Boston University. She went on to obtain a master's degree from Smith College and subsequently became a social worker. I do not recall that she ever returned home until I was about eight or nine and then only briefly, in the company of her husband. I have no early childhood memories of her.

FRED JOSEPH, JR., born in 1911, died in 1986 at age 75. I especially remember his 1930 Packard convertible coupe. It was garaged in the barn and looked as big as a fire truck to me. He joined the Army for a hitch in about 1930. After his marriage, he and his wife, Grace, lived at "552" for a time, occupying the three attic rooms—which had no kitchen or bathroom. I remember his farm in Princeton, acquired shortly thereafter. Fred

John, The Brother I Never Knew

ran heavy drop forges at the Wyman-Gordon Company. He suffered a crippling industrial accident which would have left most men bed-ridden. By sheer grit and determination he became mobile again.

(EUNICE) OLIVE, born in 1909 and our family's most accomplished pianist, was named after my mother's sister. I still reminisce over my visit to Boston with her which included my first trip on a train. We toured the *U.S.S. Constitution* (Old Ironsides) in Charlestown, and ate lunch in the elegant Locke Ober's—my first restaurant experience.

(MILDRED) PEARL was born in 1913. She and I still josh each other concerning our true age; easy to do since we are ten years apart by birth. Pearl, a pragmatic person, was my childhood advisor concerning the merits of starting a bank savings account earning interest and thereby establishing a nest-egg for some special need or occasion.

GLADYS MINERVA, born in 1915, was probably named for Ma's cousin, Gladys (MacPhee) Miller. Her creative, artistic bent heightened my awareness of aesthetic beauty all around me. She and Pearl were very close, shared a bedroom, and often went on exotic vacations to faraway places unknown to most of us.

CHARLES HOWARD, named after Dr. Marston, our family doctor of early days, was born in 1916. Charlie was my athlete role-model even though I could never equal his natural ability in sports. He was known as an outstanding short-stop and left field home-run hitter on the Tatnuck School baseball team.

RICHARD STANLEY, born in 1918, died in 1985 at 67 years of age. Dick had a sonorous baritone voice. He was a frequent soloist at church services, weddings and other occasions. He had a natural ear for music and taught himself to play the ukulele, guitar, piano and organ. Girls were attracted to him because of his handsome features and debonair manner, both enhanced by his elegant mode of dress.

PHYLLIS JUNE, born in 1920, was the sibling with whom I was closest during childhood. We sometimes pretended we were the Bobbsey Twins, or Bunny Brown and his sister Sue, and shared our innermost thoughts, a circumstance I shall always treasure.

ELIZABETH MARY, born in 1926, was my pretty, talented baby sister, as she was to us all. Betty and I participated in a number of church plays and operettas. We also played piano duets at recitals. I always beat her to the finish of *The William Tell Overture* by at least two measures!

I, JAMES MALCOLM, the baby boy, was born in 1923 and named after Ma's father, James, as well as her grandfather James MacPhee, and her favorite book of the Bible, *The Epistle of James*. "Malcolm" was to honor Scotland's first king. I weighed into this world at 10 pounds, 8 ounces, a heavy burden for Ma then, and in later years in other ways as well!

Because of the long span of twenty-one years (1905 to 1926) during which we eleven children were born, it felt to me as if we were more like three families of children, each of which grew up in situations at home and abroad quite different from those the other two experienced. In a sense, the first group (John, Eva, Olive and Fred) were more like aunts and uncles to me. Their childhood memories would have included the historically significant people, places and events of the decade 1910 to 1920. These were undoubtedly discussed in school and at home, e.g.: the 1915 sinking of the *S.S. Lusitania* by a German U-boat and the entrance of the United States into World War I in 1917; the election of Woodrow Wilson as President in 1912, replacing Teddy Roosevelt; the adoption of Income Tax laws in 1913; the election of James Michael Curley as Mayor of Boston in 1914; the opening of the Panama Canal in 1914; the Russian Revolution of 1917 under Lenin's leadership; women winning the right to vote in 1920.

They witnessed the commercial development of airplanes, and the replacement of horse and buggies with automobiles as common modes of transportation. Child labor in mills and factories, mines and farms, and in domestic service was still a common practice.

The middle group (Pearl, Gladys, Charles and Richard) seemed more like typical older sisters and brothers. In many ways they were role models for us who would follow and had a stronger influence on the development of our interests, our social graces, dress codes and habits of work and play. The current events of the day with which they were familiar were also known to us. Their heroes and villains in public affairs were ours as well.

Sister Pearl recalls winter days in the early 1920's when Fred drove Eva, Olive, Gladys and her in the one-horse open sleigh to Miss Halliday's house for their piano lessons. While one of them sat at the keyboard the others played checkers or read in Miss Halliday's parlor while awaiting their turn. I presume Brother John and Pa must have helped Fred hitch up the horse to the sleigh for this weekly adventure.

Phyllis, Betty and I were the last group—kid sisters and a kid brother. We developed close bonds to each other during childhood. Our school days and other growing-up experiences were well known to each other. We were children of the Great Depression of the 1930's. Our older brothers' and sisters' childhood years were spent in the more prosperous times of the previous two decades.

CHAPTER II

Home

The House—"552"

HOME WAS MORE THAN THE HOUSE we lived in. It encompassed the barn, gardens and yards; and the fields, woods, swamps, and pond where so many of our hours and days were spent.

Our house, built at the turn of the century, was of rambling Victorian architecture with front and back roofed "piazzas" (porches), a castellated front turret, two gables sheathed in clapboards and shingles, "gingerbread" trim along the eaves, and wooden window shutters that really could be shut to provide summer shade or opened to let winter sunlight in. It was painted brown with yellow trim. We referred to it fondly as "552," and still do.

It had ten rooms. The kitchen, dining room, living room and parlor, as well as the bathroom, pantry and a large formal front hall were on the first floor. The three second-floor bedrooms and hall were reached by a balustrade staircase. Three more bedrooms were located in the finished attic with its dormered windows and slanted ceilings. Closets were few and small.

All rooms were wallpapered and carpeted, except for the painted walls and linoleum floors of the kitchen, bathroom and attic rooms. Curtains hung at all windows. Steam heat radiators warmed the first two floors. We had no storm windows—they were almost unheard of in those times. The large four-pane windows fit loosely in their tracks, rattling and admitting cold drafts in fierce gales of winter. In this season we stuffed old socks and other rags around their frames with a kitchen knife. Magical, intricate and delicate frost crystal scenes grew on the panes:

"522"—The Kemp Camelot

ferns, tropical forests, clouds, animals, birds. When sunlight struck them they became shot through with all colors of the prism—like church windows! As we all knew very well, these works of art were created by the long pointed fingers of Jack Frost when no one was watching!

The black cast-iron Glenwood stove with its chrome trim and pipes dominated the kitchen. The several round lids—one had lids within lids—could be removed for more direct heat on pots and pans. Countless pies, cakes and loaves of bread, each with its own tantalizing aroma, passed through the oven door. Tongues of flame leapt up from the open lids when wood—or sometimes anthracite coal—was added to the firebox. Daily chores included the shaking down and removal of ashes, and replenishing the wood box which stood by the stove in response to Ma's request, "James, please bring in another armful of wood." The wooden ice chest sat in the pantry, just beyond the cast-iron sink. Its drip pan needed constant emptying on summer days. Ben Mountain, the iceman, delivered new cakes of ice which had been cut from Mill Pond or Patch's Pond the previous winter.

A copper hot-water tank stood in its own closet just off the pantry, storing hot water from kitchen stove coils and thus providing heated water to the bathroom. Occasionally, when the kitchen fire raged too fiercely, the water turned to steam, causing the boiler to rumble ominously.

From the vantage point of the wooden kitchen table and chairs—just inside the door and under the south-facing windows—we looked out to the back porch ("piazza") through bittersweet and wisteria vines. Beyond lay the side yard with its lavender and white lilacs, forsythias and two cherry trees. The first robins and bluebirds of spring nested in their branches. In winter, we peered through long, pointed icicles to the drifted snow covering the lawns and cornfields.

The dining room, where all evening meals, Sunday dinner and holiday feasts were taken, was furnished with a large rectangular oak table, matching chairs, a sideboard and, in winter, a black, round cast-iron stove. A sepia-tinted reproduction of *Christ's Last Supper* hung over the sideboard.

The living room and parlor could be combined or separated by sliding paneled wooden doors which disappeared into the walls. Olive's grand piano, which had replaced the upright piano, was the focal point of the living room. Its furnishings also included several upholstered chairs, a couch, and a console model Philco radio. Family evenings, as well as Sunday afternoons, were spent here or in the kitchen.

Use of the parlor was reserved for entertaining company. Windows looked out on the south and east yard hedges and lilacs, and to the front "piazza." Framed floral prints hung on the parlor walls. It was furnished with upholstered and caned chairs, decorative mahogany tables and, within the turret-corner, an upholstered bench. The wind-up console model Victrola also sat in the turret. Its shelves were filled with 78-rpm Bakelite RCA Victor recordings of operatic ballads sung by Enrico Caruso and Jenny Lind, Scottish ballads sung by John McCormack and Harry Lauder, and other vocal classics. The bamboo or steel needles for the playing arm were kept in little silver cylindrical containers. Earlier, brother Fred's crystal set was kept here. This predecessor to the radio was a magical thing. By moving a hairlike wire into the pits of a small silver disc, we could hear voices or music from far away through the ear phones attached to it.

A paneled door led to the front hall and thereby to the front door with its brass hardware. A large oak bookcase with glass doors stood here, filled with the complete works of Dickens and other classics. The black Bakelite upright model telephone on its stand, three wood-framed and upholstered occasional chairs, the gold-framed mirror and an Oriental rug completed the hall furnishings. Halfway up the staircase a decorative window with multi-colored glass panels surrounding it—yellow, orange, red, blue, green—looked northward to the sharp bend in Chandler Street leading to Tatnuck Square. The second floor hall, sometimes used as my bedroom, led to the three double occupancy bedrooms. The large and gracious front room—in which we were all born—with its turret corner and elegant windows was, in my memory, occupied variously by Olive, Pearl and Gladys, rather than Ma and Pa. In later years I wondered why Ma and Pa did not retain this as their room.

The south room over the living room was used at different times by Gladys, Phyllis and Betty, and the north room over the dining room was assigned to Charlie and Dick. The attic staircase and the "little attic" over the kitchen were entered from this room. My room was either the upstairs hall or the north attic room with its dormered window. Phyllis and Betty occupied the south attic room for some of their earlier years. Ma and Pa apparently moved to the front attic room as the family grew. We were curious as to what might be in the attic of the turret at the corner of this room. It was walled over and inaccessible.

The front piazza with its hanging swing seat—later replaced by the glider couch—was a delightful place to spend summer evenings listening to the last calls of birds, observing the subtle light changes from dusk to dark, and watching the occasional traffic move along Chandler Street. It was always cool and shaded here even on the hottest days of July and August. The piazza also provided an ideal vantage point from which to tend our vegetable stand while at the same time reading a favorite book.

The earthen-floored cellar with its fieldstone foundation walls was a dark, musty and sometimes mysterious place. Cobwebs hanging from the floor joists startled us as they brushed our faces. The big steam boiler-furnace with its asbestos-clad pipes radiating from it held a central place.

The unheated milk room—attached to the back wall of the house and reached by a separate outside door—had been the headquarters of Pa's Maple Grove Dairy until it failed during the Depression. It was now occasionally used as a supplemental bedroom. I slept here, as did Ma and Pa, during those two years that Fred, Grace and Suzanne lived in the three attic rooms.

All in all, despite the frugal financial resources of our family during my childhood years, the accoutrements of our home bespoke a gracious way of life, a mystique that has marked us all.

What childhood treasures, works of art, school work papers, secret notes to oneself or to others, photographs, autograph books, valentines, May-day baskets, lie where they were placed so many years ago in a far reach of an attic closet, under floorboards, or in wall partitions, still undiscovered by later occupants of "552"? These walls and hidden artifacts might tell a tale worth hearing of a family's life in the first half of the twentieth century, of people now gone from this place or from the world and now forgotten except for those who knew them well. These same walls might give back the sounds of soliloquies, dialogues, deep thoughts, questions, conjectures, sounds of merriment, of music, of laughter, of hopes and fears, and of tragedies, all of which were the warp and woof of our lives.

The Barn

The barn was a vestige from the days of horse and buggy transportation as well as farm and field work. It stood at the end of our driveway just beyond the house. Upon entering through its heavy sliding door you caught sight of two empty horse stalls and the hay-loft reached by a ladder. Horse collars, harnesses and other tack equipment still hung from pegs although they had not been used for many years. The buggies, sleighs and wagons were gone by the time of my youth, but traces of them could be seen in the heavy plank floor. Some hay, grain and oats still could be found in corners. It still smelled musty, as a barn should, particularly on damp days. The cellar had been cleared of its accumulation of manure. Although the barn was dismantled during the depression years, the floor was left in place for a year or two, allowing the cellar to be used as a chicken coop. Still later, the floor was removed and the hole filled, the resulting area being used temporarily as a boxing/wrestling arena!—and finally a flower garden.

The Yards

A brick walk led to the front piazza from the street. Two gigantic poplar trees eighty or more feet in height along with a majestic oak stood along the front boundary. Baltimore orioles built their swinging basket nests in their branches. We knew we were almost home when we caught sight of these sentinels.

The poplars blew down in the 1936 hurricane. The house never seemed quite the same afterwards. However, they did provide furnace firewood for two winters. Uncle Fred chopped them into firewood with his two-edged lumberman's axe, using the skills of his lumberjack father. I presume Uncle Fred had practiced this craft himself as a young Nova Scotian. He switched from blade to blade at the top of each stroke, his axe ringing like a church bell as it bit into the wood. As he began each wedge-shaped cut he created chips two feet or more in width. I was in awe of this mighty display of raw muscle power and tried to copy his technique in my backyard wood pile.

Flower gardens bloomed between the driveway and the south side of the house. This is where Ma always planted her pansies—her favorite flower. My earliest memory, perhaps at three years of age, is of her holding my hand there while in the other hand she held a woven basket full of pansies about to be planted. A sloping lawn led to the two cherry trees—one bearing red fruit and the other purple—forsythias, lilac bushes, and several bird houses. Two acres of cornfield lay beyond. In the summer we could walk unseen between the rows of corn, smell the sweet corn tassels and gaze at white clouds sailing across the blue sky overhead. In October, after the harvest, we made tepees from the dry shocks. They were warmed by the sun, and breezes rustled through their leaves. They became our own domain where we could just sit and think our own private thoughts for a time while breathing in the warm musty smell of autumn.

To the northward lay Almgrens' yard, separated from ours by a high stone wall and ranks of lilacs, forsythias and elderberries.

More lawns and flower gardens lay behind our house including a profusion of hollyhocks growing on the bank where the barn had once stood. The gardens on the former barn site were in semi-formal style, with stone and sea-shell walks leading through gladiolus, peonies, cosmos, zinnias and petunias. Charlie was the chief designer and cultivator of this area—a job later inherited by me. The family often sat in this back yard garden on balmy evenings to watch the sun set in the western sky.

The Fields, Woods and Pond

Beyond the back yard lay the vegetable gardens, woods, and a series of fields and swamps. An old overgrown logging road led to Patch's Pond through stands of scrub oak and maple, and fields where wild flowers grew. Buttercups—you could tell from the reflected yellow color of a buttercup held under the chin if someone liked butter—bluets, daisies, violets, devil's paintbrush were found in profusion here. Myriads of butterflies and bees fed on their pollen during the daylight hours, and fireflies traced their eerie paths above them through the darkness of August nights. We flew home-made kites here made from sticks and Christmas wrapping paper, with old socks or rags for tails.

The swamps were populated by frogs, garter and black snakes, painted and box turtles—and monstrous snapping turtles. Skunk cabbage, jack-in-the-pulpits, pussy-willows, laurel, sumac and stands of maples and birches grew on the banks. Whip-poor-wills called from their shadows at sunset. Mayflowers, lady slippers, checkerberries, blueberries and Solomon's seals grew in the drier, sunlit rises along the way.

One branch of The Fork, where four paths met, led through a grove of tall pines to The Point, a finger extending into the pond. On the way you passed The Cove where water lilies floated on the surface, and bass and perch lurked beneath. Crawfish, those grey translucent miniature lobsters, and fresh-water clams could be found around and under the stones at the water's edge.

From The Point you could look across about a hundred feet of water to where the city kids gathered. Groups of them would pass "552" before mid-morning, having walked three or four miles from their hot tenement houses to spend the day at Patch's Pond. They proceeded down Glendale Street—a rough path leading to The Fork—and on to their side of The Point. They sounded strangely foreign to us as they conversed in loud, explosive tones. They never swam across to our side of The Point, and we seldom ventured onto their territory. Perhaps both groups were equally wary of the other, and so a territorial confrontation never occurred. In other directions we saw The Island, the Dam Cove, Ice House Point, and in the distance, the

Mill Street shore. As our swimming skills and stamina increased, these destinations represented progressive challenges to be conquered.

CHAPTER III

Family Life:
Food, Shelter
And Clothing

Our Daily Bread

WE ATE AT HOME. Restaurants, diners and sandwich shops were unknown to us as children. Our food, whether a snack or a meal, was taken with proper dishes, flatware, cups and saucers, glasses, cloth napkins and tablecloths—and good manners. No paper products were utilized. Breakfast was eaten in the kitchen, often in shifts as dictated by the requirements of the day—school, work, or maintenance of the household. The usual fare was oatmeal or other hot grain cereals, toast, jam, tea or coffee, occasionally supplemented by boiled or scrambled eggs. Dinner—the noon-time week-day meal—was typically a sandwich from home, eaten at work or at school and often spread with the "leftovers" of the night before. In summertime it frequently included tomatoes, cucumbers and lettuce from our garden. Saturday's dinner might consist of home-made soups or hot tomato juice, baked bean and ketchup sandwiches, or perhaps fried hash patties of mashed potatoes, carrots, beets and ground-up meat. We always ate supper—the evening meal—as a family around the dining-room table. Its staple was potatoes, hand-mashed with butter and milk, or sometimes boiled. Brother Charlie was the undisputed family expert in creating creamy mashed potatoes. I delighted in creating ponds in them and filled them with melted butter or gravy. Our repast was completed with a variety of fresh vegetables from the garden—summer squash, sweet corn, tomatoes, cucumbers, beets, carrots, onions, cabbage—or in winter, "canned" vegetables from Mason jars put up by Ma the previous fall. Stacks of bread, often homemade, along with whatever flesh we could afford—chicken, fish, liver, hamburg, ham, or pot roast—completed our evening meal. We drank water during the meal, with tea—"Aunt Eva's" weak tea for kids—at its conclusion. Infrequently, we might have dessert—applesauce, rhubarb, a cake or pie baked by Ma or one of my sisters. Our "butter" was Nucoa, prepared from a block of white unappetizing margarine into which we mixed a capsule of yellow-orange coloring. Once tinted, its appeal improved immeasurably. I suppose as a relatively low-cholesterol corn-oil product it was even better for us than real butter.

Olive, Pearl and Gladys from time to time would eat supper at the kitchen table with Phyllis, Betty or me, sometimes all three, for purposes of instructing us in proper table manners and other matters of etiquette. All dishes were hand-washed, dried and put away as a communal affair around the pantry sink. The small kids were the dryers and polishers. Hot water was supplied from the copper tank or from the large kettle which sat on the stove.

Tea-Time

Just about anytime could be tea time, taken with toast spread with homemade jellies, jams, cinnamon and sugar, honey, Brer Rabbit molasses, or marmalade from Dundee, Scotland. On occasion one of my sisters might have baked cookies—or even Scotch scones. Tea was steeped in a china pot by pouring roiling, boiling water over the loose tea leaves—Salada orange pekoe and pekoe—swirling the pot to extract the optimum flavor. The resultant brew was decanted through a silver strainer into our decorative, fragile china cups with saucers. Younger children were served "Aunt Eva's tea"—mostly hot water, sugar and milk with a teaspoon of tea. Now and then Ma would read the tea leaves which remained in our cups, always foretelling the good fortune or adventure which would soon be ours. Toast was made on top of the kitchen or dining room wood-stove by placing slices directly on the hot lids or on the four-sided slotted tin toaster which sat on the stove top. In summertime, tea might be replaced by hand-squeezed fresh lemonade cooled with ice shaved from the ice-box, or our home-made root beer. Carbonated beverages were almost unknown except for ginger ale as a special treat when you were sick.

Shopping for Food

Food that we could not raise or harvest ourselves was bought in bulk wherever possible—sometimes from the Salem Square farmers' market or directly from farms. Southwick's farm and orchard was one of my favorites because a visit to their place provided me another opportunity to gaze with fascination at Mr. Southwick's appendix, preserved in a jar of alcohol and exhibited on the fireplace mantel of their living room. It looked like a huge, fat, pale nightcrawler. Their farm was on Bailey Road in

Leicester. On the way we passed Brigg's farm and two or three others whose fields are now the site of the Worcester Metropolitan Airport. Proceeding further north on these country dirt roads, we would stop at MacHale's dairy farm in Paxton. They were very friendly folks toward kids as well as with our parents. Even their cows and two collie dogs seemed friendly and contented as they wandered through the barn-yard.

On Friday evenings Ma and Pa would buy other staples at Brockelmann's Worcester Market, always accompanied by two or three of us children. It was probably the original supermarket although that phrase hadn't been invented yet. Here you could buy bulk quantities of vegetables, canned goods, crackers, butter, cheese, dried apricots, raisins and prunes, fresh fruit, nuts, and even hermit cookies (gingerbread with raisins) from burlap bags, barrels and cartons.

Along with the Mason-jar home-canned tomatoes, peaches, applesauce, jellies, jams, mince-meat, piccalilli and other relishes, winter squash, potatoes, carrots, beets, turnips, and cabbages were stored in our cellar as winter supplies.

Emergency measures were called for when the provender of the pantry shelves could not provide for the next day's breakfast. In those dire circumstances, we were forced to seek temporary relief from the old-time grocery stores at Tatnuck Square or June Street—the A&P or the First National—all within walking distance; but never Taft's Market which catered only to families of means and which always charged a few cents more for any item. Family emissaries were dispatched with a limited amount of coinage in hand to these purveyors of essential staples: Quaker Oats in the cylindrical box with a smiling Quaker on the label, Nabisco Shredded Wheat in the box with the spectacular illustration of Niagara Falls, a five-pound bag of flour, Domino sugar, or salt. The white-aproned grocer would retrieve these articles—usually from the top shelves—with a long-handled hook held in one hand while he deftly caught the package in the other. The bill was figured right on the paper bag with a pencil stored behind the grocer's ear and wetted in his mouth to assure the numbers were black enough to read. It was impolite to check his arithmetic at the counter but we always did upon returning home.

While in the A&P or First National, I stared in wonder at the mouth-watering delicacies displayed in their vegetable and fruit bins: huge bunches of bananas from Honduras, cantaloupes, navel oranges and grapefruit from Florida, dates from Mediterranean countries, iceberg lettuce, celery, carrots, beets, and exotic squashes from the Imperial Valley of California, purple, blue and green grapes from some tropical land, large smooth-skinned potatoes from Idaho. I had learned about these far-away places—about their crops and food-stuffs—in my geography lessons, but never really understood the reality of these places until I saw their products with my very own eyes.

Boxes of Nabisco biscuits and cookies were arrayed rank-on-rank along the aisles, each with its glass cover. Steaks, pork chops, ham slices, and sausages filled the trays of the meat counters, flanked by blocks of cheeses from Vermont, Wisconsin and even Holland. I wondered if anyone actually bought these provisions and what they might taste like—or were they just items for display?

Saturday night at the Hathaway Bakery was another food gathering festive occasion. Stale products—bread, pastries and other baked goods—could be bought for fifty cents a bag on a cash and carry, bring-your-own-bag basis. We used a canvas Muir's Laundry bag because it could hold two or three bushels.

Upon returning to "552," we sorted this bounty in the kitchen by type and relative freshness—breads, doughnuts, cupcakes, pies, frosted cakes. The dessert categories were consumed in a day or two; the stalest bread became bread pudding or french toast. At those times when we had neither a car nor the gasoline to run it, Pa would walk the two miles to the bakery and return with the bag over his shoulder, following paths through woods and fields to avoid embarrassing his family and himself.

Maple Syrup

Late February and early March, when temperatures rose above freezing during the day and dropped to below freezing at night, heralded the maple sap season. For several years Charlie and Dick, assisted by me, tapped twenty or thirty sugar maple trees, most of them not on our property, hammered hand-made willow-branch spigots into the tap-holes and hung out our buckets. These were emptied into large milk cans left over from Pa's milk business. We shifted from #10 cans to glass bottles and jugs after competitive sap collectors punched holes in our cans with ice-picks. The glass containers in turn were promptly smashed. We responded in kind by destroying our competitors' equipment. This unseen battle escalated to taps being broken off and holes plugged. Although we never knew for certain who the sap raiders were, we had made pretty close guesses based on the direction of foreign footsteps in the snow.

Our sap was boiled down in large pans on the kitchen stove, producing a family supply of maple syrup. Bearing in mind that it took at least thirty-two quarts of sap to make one quart of syrup, great clouds of hot steam were generated which tended to steam wallpaper off the walls as well as create minor rainstorms as it condensed on the ceiling, to the chagrin of Ma and my older sisters who might just have re-papered the dining room. The whole maple sap enterprise finally came to a halt for two reasons: Ma and the girls voiced stronger and stronger objections to the unsightly wrinkles in the wall paper, and, more importantly, our unseen sap enemies took to peeing in our buckets, making any future syrup suspect. We converted to a substitute made from Mapoline artificial flavoring—it came in a small bottle with a blue label—mixed into a warm slurry of sugar and water. It was passable on pancakes or french toast, and besides, there was no way we could afford real store-bought Vermont maple syrup.

One of the delights of July and August was to pick a tomato or cucumber in the garden and devour it right there while it was still warm and retained its delicate spicy smell and taste—qualities which quickly dissipated. Another was to pick the first ripe ears of golden bantam corn, shuck them on the back porch, drop them into the waiting pot of boiling water, and eat them for supper—all in less than an hour from stalk to stomach. We even sucked the last sweet flavor from the cobs when the kernels were gone!

This was also the season when we made root beer from a solution of sugar and water flavored with Baker's extract—with the Indian on the label—and fermented with a cake of Fleischman's yeast. It was bottled, stoppered and stored in the cellar until it became effervescent. Occasionally a stopper exploded, followed by a rush down the cellar stairs to reinforce the plugs in the remaining bottles. When it was declared "done," we could hardly wait to taste this cool frothy beverage which far exceeded in taste any store-bought carbonated imitation.

On rare summer weekends we made home-made strawberry, raspberry or blueberry ice cream in the wooden-bucket, hand-cranked freezer from a quart or two of heavy cream and fresh berries picked that day. The ingredients were placed in a metal container surrounded by chipped ice and rock salt. This mixture was turned by relays of kids until it was stiff and ready to eat. I have never had ice cream that equalled it.

The Ice-Man

Our refrigeration needs were met by Ben Mountain who made ice deliveries for the Tatnuck Ice Company. Their ice was cut from Mill Pond or Patch's Pond. Ben was aptly named. He was a mountain of a man. His handle-bar moustache was stained by smoke which arose from a corn-cob pipe clenched tightly between his teeth. We never called Ben, "Ben" to his face. He was always Mr. Mountain to us.

His steel-rimmed wooden-wheeled ice wagon was neatly painted with the house-colors of ice-blue with white trim. It was drawn by two powerful, majestic horses—they may have been Clydesdales. Their harnesses were polished; their bronze hardware shone brightly. Ben cut chunks of ice from the massive blocks which were stored in his wagon, weighing them on a bronze scale which hung above the tail gate. He bore our ice, held with ice-tongs, on his rubber-matted back as he mounted our back steps to the kitchen and proceeded to the pantry ice chest. Ill-fitting blocks were shaped with a few deft strokes of his ice-pick. There were always two or three of us kids standing around as he returned to his wagon. We hoped to receive a few slivers of ice to suck on and we were never denied.

Ben often paused in front of our house to feed and water his team—oats and grain from canvas bags hung around his horses' necks, water from a pail stored under his bench. These needs satisfied, he hoisted the heavy dome-shaped iron anchor which had kept his team from straying, gave a tug on the reins and a couple of "cluck-cluck" commands, and they were off and away, the horses' hooves clop-clopping on the pavement. Their passage was frequently marked by two piles of horse-buns. Flocks of crows, blackbirds and sparrows feasted on the un-digested grain so deposited. He called on us much less frequent-ly in the wintertime for two reasons. The ice melted much more slowly, and we supplemented our ice needs with the large icicles which hung from the back porch gutters—some two feet or more in length and at least four inches thick.

The Ice Man—Ben Mountain and His Team

Garbage and Trash

Garbage and trash disposal—those twin blights of modern ur-ban and suburban life—never presented a problem to us. There was no municipal garbage and trash pick-up service since there was no need for it. Neither were we aware of a municipal dump or landfill available to households. In the environmentalist lingo of today, we re-cycled everything—sometimes three or four times—and buried the few degradable remnants. Those major generators of trash—non-degradable plastics—were still in the developmental stage as technological curiosities. Our only acquaintances with them were as Bakelite telephones and 78 r.p.m. records. Junk-mail pollution by the bushel was an abomination of the future, thank goodness.

Left-over food was often served in an altered form for another meal or used for sandwich spreads, hash, stew or soup. Stale bread and cake were converted to bread pudding or french toast. Apple peelings became apple jelly, and orange and lemon peels, marmalade. Any remaining food scraps were fed to the chickens. Worn-out clothes, blankets, sheets or towels were put to new uses as dust cloths, floor-washing mops, insulation around drafty windows and doors, or as hooked or braided rugs. Strings of all sizes and colors were retrieved from bundles and added to the expanding string ball which sat on a pantry shelf. Its many uses included tying up tomato plants, pea and bean vines, and morning glories to supporting sticks. Old clotheslines and lengths of other ropes were coiled and stored in the cellarway, thus extending their life toward future needs. Newspapers, store-wrappings, paper bags, cardboard boxes and other paper products were fed to the stove or furnace to generate a few free calories. Corn stalks, along with tree and shrub prunings and brush, were burnt in late fall in the cornfield. The wood ashes made good fertilizer, and corn borer eggs were destroyed at the same time. Old lumber was used for home repairs or as fire wood. Bent nails were straightened and used again. Scrap metal—old automobile parts, pots and pans, broken stove grates, old iron or copper pipes—was saved to sell to the ragman.

The Rag-Man

We never knew his name or where he lived. He served us for two useful purposes. We disposed of junk while making a dollar or two in the process—a transaction that was profitable to him as well. He appeared every spring and fall. His plaintive, quavering call of "ra-a-a-a-ags, ra-a-a-a-a-gs" announced his approach along Chandler Street. Except for his white shirt, he was dressed all in black—wide-brimmed felt hat, necktie, knee-length frock coat, baggy pants and heavy-soled shoes. He was gaunt of frame and his grey, scraggly, pointed beard hung half-way to his waist; his long unkempt hair covered his ears and neck. The wheels of his rickety old wagon canted out at four different angles; a weighing scale hung over its tailgate. The whole contraption was drawn by a poor, skinny old plug of a horse. The horse and his master were well matched.

Despite these outward appearances, the rag-man drove a hard bargain as we haggled over the price of our scrap metal, newspapers, rags, bottles and broken tools. He was wily, and wary of all attempts to deceive or cheat him. This was made very clear the time Charlie and Dick had soaked the middle layer of their newspaper bundles to increase their weight; and on another occasion when they had inserted several layers of scrap asphalt shingles. He judged accurately what these bundles should weigh, and after pointing out this deceit in a high-pitched nasal tone, reluctantly paid them at a "dry paper weight" rate.

Morning Time and Evening Time

Ma and Pa were up and about before dawn while their children slept. After some alone time together they made morning coffee or tea, hot cereal, set the kitchen breakfast table, and ate an early breakfast. Lunch sandwiches were made and packed for eight children. A tight schedule was required for use of the one bathroom, averaging about three minutes for each person for all necessary functions. This pressure was lessened by a shared-time arrangement whereby two or three girls or two boys might occupy it at the same time. The working girls—Olive, Pearl, and Gladys—with a 7:30 bus to catch, had priority at about 6:45 followed by Charlie and Dick who, in later years, had their own cars as they departed for their jobs. The three school kids— Phyllis, Betty and I—used the facilities after 7:30, followed by our breakfast. One of my morning duties was to stand half-way up the front stairs looking out the decorative window for the bus rounding the corner and to sound the alarm, " here comes the bus." At this signal, Olive, Pearl and Gladys would bolt through the front door, often with coffee and toast in hand which was retrieved by Ma as they boarded for their day as secretaries at the State Mutual Life Assurance Company.

The living room was the center of many family activities. Phyllis, Betty and I practiced daily at Olive's grand piano after school, followed by inside or outside chores and neighborhood yard games before our older brothers and sisters returned home from their jobs. We tuned into fifteen-minute daily or weekly kids' radio shows before supper—"Little Orphan Annie," "Jack Armstrong, The All-American Boy," "The Ralston Straight Shooters." The family gathered around the Philco after supper for "Fibber Magee and Molly," "Snow Village," "Amos 'n Andy," "Jack Benny," "Fred Allen" or "The Shadow." Any school homework or special projects were completed around the dining room table following these entertainments. When stormy weather kept us indoors on summer or winter evenings, we might play Old Maid, Checkers, Game of India or Parcheesi in the dining room—although never on Sunday! Ma's fingers never rested. It was also in these evening hours that her knitting needles produced an endless supply of mittens, stockings, sweaters, hats and scarves to protect her children from the winter's cold.

Ma and Pa often sat by the kitchen stove reading to each other—mostly Psalms or other Old Testament books prior to retiring by or before nine-thirty. Bed-time for the three youngest children was also about nine o'clock. As we departed for our beds on the coldest nights of winter, we carried a warm brick which had been heated in the oven and wrapped in a towel. This was placed under our blankets to keep our feet warm. All family members were kissed and hugged with reciprocal wishes for sweet dreams— and Ma's reminder to "say your prayers." We did so before falling asleep—"Now I Lay Me Down to Sleep" complete with all family names, and The Lord's Prayer. Our older brothers and sisters stayed up until ten-thirty or even eleven o'clock reading or listening to the radio. The girls completed beauty treatments and enjoyed a last tea and toast before retiring.

I do not recall that the telephone ever rang or that calls were made by the family during my childhood. It sat silent on its table in the hall. Perhaps it was disconnected during the depression years. Its use may have been reserved for emergency local calls to a doctor or the fire or police departments. I doubt that any long-distance call was ever made or received, although I had heard that such things were possible.

The Church in Our Lives

Wesley Methodist Episcopal Church was a central focus of our family life. This Gothic stone structure was of cathedral proportions. The sanctuary was resplendent with stained glass epitomized by a magnificent rose window in the rear balcony. A four-manual pipe organ dominated the chancel, complemented by antiphonal organs in the three balconies. Situated in the city, the

Wesley Methodist Episcopal Church

church was one of several imposing buildings near Lincoln Square—the Courthouse, the Memorial Auditorium, the Boy's Club, and two other large, steepled churches. The distance to or from our home—about three miles—was no deterrent to our full participation in its programs. If an automobile was not available we travelled by bus or trolley car, or walked.

The 10:30 to noon Sunday service, including a twenty-minute pastoral prayer, a thirty-minute sermon, two or three choir anthems or solos and four hymns (all verses) was preceded by a half-hour senior and junior choir rehearsal for my older brothers and sisters and an hour of Sunday School for Phyllis, Betty and me. After our own Sunday School worship service, we proceeded to the balcony for the last half of the adult service, including the sermon and the grand finale choir recessional and organ postlude. The regalia of the pastor, minister of music, and choir was complemented by that of the corps of ushers in grey swallow-tailed suits, ascot ties and boutonnieres as they seated the throng, collected the offerings on gold plates and presented them at the altar—all with military precision.

For several years eight Kemps sang in the choirs, distributed among the senior, junior and children's choirs. The latter joined the others for the main service on the festive days of Easter, Thanksgiving and Christmas; otherwise, we sang occasionally at Sunday School. As one of the two or three boy soprano soloists, I performed from time to time from the chancel steps—in Latin as well as English—from the age of eight to thirteen, when my voice began its hormonally induced changes. The combined ranks of choirs—some eighty strong and fully robed—presented a processional panoply to the assembled worshipers. Upon our arrival in the chancel lofts, we had a ring-side view of the organist as he manipulated the keys of the four manuals, the foot pedals and the ranks of stops. We were frequently chided by the pastor from his exalted station in the high pulpit for unseemly, inattentive or disorderly conduct in the choir pews—particularly during his sermon.

Sunday evenings found us back at the church for the short service and hymn sing. On Wednesday evenings we attended *en masse* the spirited hymn-sing, using the green Cokesbury Hymnal and accompanied by a Chautauqua-quality pianist. From all of this hymn singing, many family favorites emerged which we all knew by heart, all verses—and in some cases still do: "When Morning Gilds The Skies," "Work for The Night is Coming," "Onward Christian Soldiers," "Faith of Our Fathers," "For the Beauty of the Earth," "Glorious Things of Thee Are Spoken," "Abide With Me," "Now the Day is Over," "Safely Through Another Week," not to mention all verses of all Christmas carols found in any hymnal. Still other evenings and Saturday mornings were reserved for meetings at the church—choir rehearsals, Boy Scout meetings, Epworth (Youth) League, and rehearsals for drama productions.

During the tenure of A. Leslie Jacobs as Minister of Music, several children's operettas were performed under his direction. I was cast in the lead role in Robin Hood, and as the father of Hansel and Gretel. Betty had the co-lead as Gretel in the latter, and was the Princess in *The Frog Prince*. I still can sing by heart several of the arias and choruses of these musicals.

Summer services were conducted by guest preachers since the pastor was on vacation for two months. The most memorable of those was Justin Laurie who delivered a real spell-binder sermon and also sang dramatic solos worthy of an operatic performance. Foremost among these was, "There Were Ninety and Nine" (sheep). Summer organ recitals were performed by E. Power Biggs before he became world-famous, as well as by our permanent organists, Mr. Jacobs and later, Donald Gilley. Summer was also the time for the annual church picnic and outing held at the Shrewsbury estate of Mr. Howard Brewer, one of our church's founding fathers and chief benefactors.

Family Rules, Codes, Values

The moral tone of our life—set by our parents—seemed to be assimilated into our lives more by example than by parental teaching and preaching, although there was some of that. We were immersed in an environment where certain types of conduct were expected; it was just "how we did things." As I look back, it seems likely that these verities may have been derived from the writings of several New England theologians and philosophers, as well as liberal doses of homespun commentaries found in the *Old Farmer's Almanac* and the commentaries of Benjamin Franklin. Some of the rules for living thus acquired as part of my New England heritage are with me still although I have not always succeeded in following these precepts, generating in turn the specter of puritanical guilt; e.g.: time is precious—use every minute for some *worthwhile* pursuit, idle fingers are the devil's tools, never put off until tomorrow what you can do today, make every step count, never carry a half-load, hard work never hurt anybody, finish what you start—half-done is not done at all. Waste not, want not, save a thing its use will come, make do—do without, fix it *before* it breaks, a stitch in time saves nine, a penny saved is a penny earned, neither a borrower nor a lender be. Clean your plate, don't waste food, there is no shame in wearing *clean* worn or patched clothes, a clean house is a healthy house, keep your body and your mind clean— they are God's temples. Use your brain and your talents otherwise they will rust and wither away, don't hide your light under a bushel, stand proud. Take care of your health—it is your best gift from your parents and God, early to bed and early to rise makes a man healthy, wealthy and wise, do not imbibe beer, wine or liquor. Laugh and the world laughs with you, cry and you cry alone, be cheerful and kind to others, be kind to dumb animals.

Pick your friends carefully—birds of a feather flock together, do not tell "fibs" (lies)—the truth will win out, do not use vulgar, foul or obscene language, or take the Lord's name in vain.

Parental discipline was mild—more in the way of chiding or admonishments than in harsh punishments. Neither parent ever laid a hand on me in anger. Birch switches on the legs were infrequently used—for good cause—and stung more emotionally than physically. Ma and Pa were supportive of discipline administered by the schools. Telling "fibs" or using slang words resulted in my mouth being washed out with soap—usually yellow laundry soap! Punishments for other offenses might also include going to bed without supper, usually tempered by tea and toast at bedtime.

No hard work inside or outside was performed on Sunday. Neither were swimming, skating, sliding, games, "jazz" or other secular radio music permitted. Broadcasts of the New York Riverside Church service and music, or strangely enough for Methodists, the inspirational sermons of Father Fulton Sheen, S.J., were encouraged. The parlor Victrola could be cranked up to play the old 78 r.p.m. Bakelite classical recordings. Sunday afternoon was a time of family entertainment as well, in the living room around Olive's grand piano. Dick, with Olive as his accompanist, would sing several selections from his repertoire: "The Holy City," "The Last Chord," "Old Man River," "Stout-Hearted Men," "Ah, Sweet Mystery of Life," "Loch Lomond." Piano solos were performed by various family "artists" depending on their present level of skill: Beethoven's "Minuet in G" or "Moonlight Sonata," Handel's "Largo" or "Sarabande," Brahms's "Waltz in A_b," "Polonaises and Waltzes" by Chopin, Schubert's "March Militaire," Schumann's "Merry Peasant," Rachmaninoff's "Prelude in C# Minor." This was also the time

Sunday After-Church Walk Time

for walks through the woods and fields or a scenic ride to surrounding towns.

Home Medicine—Ma as the Family Doctor and Nurse

Ma was the family home-remedy physician, nurse and first-aid practitioner in addition to her other roles. She ministered to us with a combination of knowledge and techniques learned from family doctors, tried-and-true remedies passed down to her by relatives and friends, and from her cousin Laura MacPhee, a registered nurse who lived in a nearby town. I do not recall that Ma or Pa were ever sick themselves. Some of her remedies, many of which I used with my own children and still apply to my own ailments, were: *chest colds/bronchitis/pneumonia*—mustard plaster powder mixed with warm water, applied to the chest and covered with a folded cloth or towel—alternate remedies were "Musterole" or Vick's "Vap-o-Rub" salve; *high fevers*—induce sweating with blankets, hot lemonade and aspirin; *common colds*—hot lemonade, aspirin and Vick's nose drops; *sore throat*—gargle made from warm water, salt and baking soda; *eye infections or irritations*—mild solution of salt, or (formerly) boric acid powder!; *coughs*—honey and lemon juice, Vick's "Vap-o-Rub" salve in a basin of boiling water with a towel over the head (a home-made humidifier); *constipation*—variously, castor oil, Epsom salt solution, cod liver oil, or rhubarb sauce in season (as a last resort, warm soapy water was administered via the enema bag—it always got explosive results!); *cuts and abrasions*—tincture of iodine, carbolic salve with bandages made of old sheets if needed; *poison ivy*—a plaster of vinegar and salt; *toothaches*—clove oil on cotton, or crushed aspirin in the cavity; *toothpaste*—a mixture of 90% baking soda and 10% salt; *sweating (smelly) feet*—soak feet in strong salt solution, scrape dead skin from soles of feet and toes with a scissor blade, dry feet vigorously with a rough towel, dust with boric acid powder; *muscular aches and pains*—Sloan's Liniment.

Dr. Marston, and later, Dr. Jewett, were called to the home for dire emergencies: childbirth, broken limbs, possible appendicitis, evidence of the serious communicable diseases of scarlet fever, diphtheria, spinal meningitis, "infantile paralysis" (polio), and at the onset of the childhood diseases—measles, mumps, chicken-pox, or fevers over 104 degrees.

Ma's diagnoses and cures were expanded upon by folk-lore passed between kids—and believed passionately. One that put me in mortal fear was that you were sure to get infantile paralysis (polio) if you shuffled through, or worse, jumped into piles of dry leaves in the fall. Death was sure to follow! Since I had already revelled in these autumnal rites, I spent several days and nights waiting for the onset of this plague. In my mind, I felt a tightening of my leg and arm muscles, my neck felt increasingly stiff, and my fingers twitched as I awaited the onset of rigor mortis.

The Dentist

We did not have regular dental check-ups as is common practice today. Neither were we acquainted with the cosmetic corrective arts of orthodontics. Except for kids from families of money, if you were born with crooked or far-spaced teeth they remained that way. Things pretty much happened as nature dictated. Baby teeth fell out one-by-one, often encouraged by constant wiggling with your tongue or with finger pressure on the loose tooth until it hung by only a strand or two of tissue. This display was a great way to alarm or annoy family members or playmates. When it finally was dislodged it was placed under our pillow at bed-time to be exchanged for a dime from the tooth-fairy. Any toothaches that Ma could not alleviate with her home-spun remedies called for a visit to the dentist—Dr. Hull or Dr.

Sleeper. My first appointment was probably in my tenth year since I had developed some gaping holes in several molars. They felt like craters of the moon when explored with the tip of my tongue and the throbbing pain they caused could no longer be controlled with crushed aspirin.

The office shared by Dr. Hull and Dr. Sleeper was located on the second floor of an old office building on Main Street, adjoining Mechanics Hall. It looked like a Norman Rockwell re-creation from the 1890's. A dark, dimly lit, narrow staircase with creaking wooden treads led to their emporium. A line of old wooden chairs in the hallway served as their reception room. No secretary or nurse was in attendance to record vital statistics and ailments; the dentists took care of these details as well. The office itself was equally dark, dreary and dusty, with dark, wood panelled walls, and creaking wooden floor boards. Two or three light bulbs hung from the high ceiling, shaded by old glass reflectors.

Both dentists were skinny and bald with steel-rimmed glasses perched on the tips of their noses. They wore short, white jackets similar to that of Mr. Curtis, the barber, and looked quite elderly, although they were probably not yet sixty years old. Dr. Sleeper attended to my needs. I, as the patient, reclined in an ancient wicker dental chair adjusted with hand levers. A long goose-neck lamp with a bare electric bulb provided illumination into my open mouth. He performed his craft with a foot-powered drill activated by a treadle and a series of exposed cables and pulleys which transferred the power to his drill. A tray holding well-worn instruments—picks, scrapers, tweezers—could be swung under my chin; a spitting tube was attached to it. A whiff of laughing gas from the rubber mask which hung from a pressure tank, or a shot of novocaine was available for excruciating pain although these ministrations were intended only for extractions.

From time to time Dr. Sleeper paused from his labors to direct a stream of cold water into my cavity from a rubber syringe, followed by the non-sequitur question, "Did that hurt a little?" as I groaned and sat bolt upright in my chair. In the end I tried to bear the pain with stoic resignation, but promised myself never to visit another dentist. Having removed the decayed matter with his assorted tools, he packed the resulting excavation variously with a pitch-like substance, dental cement or "amalgam." It seems that the practice of dentistry had not yet approached the technology of today or else Dr. Sleeper and Dr. Hull were of the old school. Most of their fillings fell out and had to be replaced in subsequent years or the offending tooth extracted after all.

Eye Glasses

Hardly anyone wore glasses during their grammar school years. I don't recall anyone in my classes who had them, although I had seen some kids on the playground who were so equipped. By and large, as with crooked teeth, you lived with what you were born with, weak eyes or not. Besides, to wear glasses was to suffer the insults of being called a sissy or "four-eyes." Moreover, glasses were considered to be somewhat of an affectation of rich kids. Many of my generation did acquire these visual aids in high school. They were considered to be "cool" in today's language, especially if they were of rimless design. I was fitted to my first pair at age sixteen, not because of any desire to improve my scholarly efforts, but simply because I could not pass my motor vehicle driving test without them!

Projects and Chores

Saturdays were largely given over to chores and projects unless the requirements of paying jobs took precedence. Although we did not follow this guideline rigidly, by and large Ma and the girls were busy with household matters while Pa and the boys were engaged in the needs of the yards and gardens. Depending on the special requirements of the season, Ma and the girls could be observed washing and repairing clothes, washing floors, dusting, cooking and baking. Pa and the boys, with occasional help from the girls depending on the time of year, concentrated on raking and mowing the lawns, trimming hedges, planting, cultivating and weeding the gardens, or cutting, splitting and sorting firewood.

All mowing and trimming, wood-cutting and splitting was done with hand-powered tools oiled and sharpened by ourselves. The scythe, with its multi-curved six-foot wooden handle and long, wide cutting blade, was a fascinating tool. We used it to cut long grass and weeds in the fields.

Our implements for cutting logs included a wooden-framed bucksaw, the blade of which was tightened with a turnbuckle, and two-man crosscut saws. One of these had a rigid, curved blade and could be used by one person if necessary. The other was far more intriguing. It was an authentic lumberjacks' saw of the type used to fell forest trees prior to the advent of power chain saws. Its flexible, six-foot blade was only 3½ inches wide, including its multi-pointed teeth. It required two people to use it properly. It only cut on "pull" strokes. While one person pulled the saw through the log, the other merely steadied and guided it without exerting any "push" pressure. Thus, the two partners alternately pulled or steadied the blade. If one applied "push" pressure this ribbon of steel would buckle and writhe like a live thing. My brothers and I enjoyed picking up the tempo of our strokes as a test of our stamina, until at last we lost the required rhythm, binding up the blade in the log. When we were really "in the groove" it felt as if we were a well-oiled machine, sort of like the drive rod of a steam locomotive.

We also repaired shoes, replacing worn soles and heels with rubber treads and glue bought at Woolworth's as a ten-cent kit. Prior to this patch work, cardboard from Shredded Wheat packages was fitted into the inside sole to temporarily cover holes which had worn through to our stockings—or feet!

Burning leaves was an annual fall ritual observed by everyone with trees in their yard. On any bright Saturday in October one could observe swirling plumes of acrid blue smoke and tongues of orange flame rising over the leaf-piles along the roadsides. I often pretended they were Indian smoke signals. The pungent odor of these pyres was a sure sign that fall had arrived, with winter not too far behind. It was a time for neighborliness as well as we remarked on each others' piles, their relative rate of combustion, exclaimed over the brilliance of the foliage, and exchanged gossip about neighborhood affairs and other bits of news. Although leaf burning is now forbidden, still it was a comparatively harmless thing to do when compared to the ton upon ton of pollutants we pour into the air today from our automobiles, trucks, airplanes, chemical factories and power plants, and from our air-conditioned homes, offices, and acre after acre of environmentally controlled stores and shopping malls.

The washing of clothes was an endless and burdensome task for Ma in those days. Soiled clothes were stirred with a wooden paddle in the copper boiler which sat on the kitchen stove. Home-made yellow soap, or Ajax, were the usual cleansing agents. This step had often been preceded by a soak in the bathtub since the two soapstone wash tubs had been removed from the kitchen. It was followed by a vigorous scrubbing with a stiff brush on the glass-ridged scrub-board. Ma performed these steps on her knees and wrung the articles by hand. We later acquired a copper-tanked electric-powered washing machine with a hand-cranked wringer, and still later, a white enamel electric washing machine with a spin-dryer! Clothes were hung to dry on long lines from the back porch, or in bad weather, wall-to-wall in the kitchen.

Ironing was done with steel irons heated on the stove to which a wooden handle could be attached. In later years Ma had an electric iron—and then a steam iron! Pants and jackets were steam pressed using a damp cloth placed over the garment. We all learned this technique as we became teen-agers interested in presenting a "sharp" image. Shirts were heavily starched, and often required the "turning" of collars and cuffs when they became frayed. School and play clothes were patched as needed. Worn sheets were cut down the middle and re-sewed on their good edges, thereby doubling their life span.

Spring cleaning on the first warm spring Saturdays of April was an all-out effort by us all, spear-headed by Ma and the girls. All floors and woodwork were scrubbed and waxed. Windows were cleaned inside and out with vinegar and/or "Bon-Ami." Carpets, rugs, mattresses, blankets, pillows, and upholstered furniture as well, were beaten and aired in the back yard. This was the usual time for re-wallpapering and painting—usually by my sisters. The boys did any critical re-painting of exterior walls, shutters, and windows, and white-washed the boulders lining the driveway and flower gardens.

Summer brought on the house-fly season at a time before combination storm and screen windows had been invented.

Window and door screens, if they existed at all, were loose fitting at best. One of the necessary tasks was to decrease the fly population by a combination of fly paper hung from the ceilings of the kitchen and porches, and fly swatters. I developed quite a marksman-like skill with the latter, often eliminating three or four flies with one quick swat.

You Can't Get There From Here—But Pa Did!

The steering mechanism of Pa's second-hand 1932 Plymouth developed some peculiar characteristics after a few years of hard miles, compounded by the effects of several aspiring drivers among his children. It would only make full turns to the right; left-hand turns were limited to a radius of no more than ten degrees. Pa needed the car to get to his night watchman job at W.P.I., a distance of some four miles and too far to walk late at night in the winter months. The money for repairs was just not available. However, being the ingenious man that he was, Pa devised an extended route whereby he could drive to W.P.I. and back making only right-hand turns. A few clock-wise circles through back streets and several backing-up maneuvers into driveways or parking lots finally led to his destination in seven or eight miles rather than four. With the arrival of springtime, enough money had been saved to get the Plymouth fixed. In addition to allowing Pa to return to a more normal commute, we were all quite pleased that the ride to church no longer took an extra half-hour.

Tending the Boiler

The steam boiler (furnace), while providing the modern convenience of central steam heat to most of the house, did require a rather high level of technical skill and art in its operation. All of us—Ma, Pa, girls, boys—quickly learned the necessary house and family survival skills required. The fire often raged too hot because of our frequent use of wood fuel rather than coal. The steam gauge at these times often reached 35 pounds or more, causing the emergency relief valve to let off a plume of steam, and a shrill scream worthy of a locomotive. All radiators would emit their own plumes, commence a heavy thumping, and the cellar would immediately fill with steam. The emergency cry of, "the steam's blowing off!" sent us flying to complete several simultaneous corrective actions: fling open the fire door, close down all dampers, if necessary shovel ashes onto the fire, open all radiator valves, add cold water to the boiler. The latter action, if overdone, caused hot water to erupt from the radiators in addition to the steam. Why the boiler did not explode and exit through the roof on one of these occasions escapes me. However, this problem was alleviated from time to time as finances permitted by the purchase of coal—sometimes anthracite, sometimes bituminous—which burned at a steady, predictable rate.

Chickens in the Yard—and in the Little Attic

We kept a flock of chickens, usually fifty or so, as our source of fresh eggs, and from time to time, meat. They roosted in the barn cellar with the fenced back yard as their range. They also served as mobile garbage disposal units, thus reducing the amount of commercial feed needed. From time to time Pa would select a non-productive hen or a rooster for our next supper. Part of this necessary but gruesome process was the chopping off of its head with an axe wielded by Pa. The poor headless bird hopped and flopped around the yard for a minute or so as we watched with rapt fascination. The body was immediately dunked by the feet in a pail of boiling water, followed by the plucking of the feathers—especially the blue "pin feathers"—by us children. I can still recall the warm musty smell of wet feathers as we bent to this task.

The "Little Attic"—over the kitchen and entered by a low door from Charlie and Dick's room—served for two or three winters as a brooder for about two hundred newly hatched chicks. Heat rising from the kitchen stove warmed its floor. Pa picked up these hatchlings at the Union Square Railroad Station. They came in cardboard boxes with round air vents punched in their sides.

They were fed and watered in the Little Attic for two or three months until they had acquired real feathers, and the warmer weather would allow them to survive out-of-doors. It was intriguing to hear their chorus of "peeps," but they did require constant daily care: water bottles and mash trays filled, droppings onto newspapers removed, disposing of those which might have died during the night. I shared these duties with my brothers.

As the chicks grew older their odors became stronger and their voices more strident, to the consternation of my older sisters who, more and more, were developing an air of worldly-wise sophistication. The girls' objections rose to higher decibel levels on those occasions when they had visitors, particularly boyfriends who might inquire, "Do I hear chickens?" It was a tough act for them to maintain their composure at those times.

However, this source of their embarrassment was shortly to come to an end. It required a considerable sense of balance to walk along the floor joists while caring for those chicks without stepping between the timbers and onto the kitchen ceiling lathes and plaster. I recall vividly a mis-step followed by my right foot and leg crashing through the ceiling. There I was with my leg suspended over the hot stove, and plaster, chicken droppings and other debris scattered over the kitchen floor and stove. This event quickly led to the demise of the Little Attic chicken farm!

Family Festivals and Celebrations

Christmastime was that wondrous blend of religious images and experiences surrounding the celebration of the birth of Jesus and the secular mystery, magic and myth of the yuletide season. The prevailing spirit of thoughtfulness, kindness, generosity and love was much with us then.

Our Christmas tree was usually cut from the woods by Pa or my brothers. In some years it might be a white pine or hemlock. It was set up in the parlor and elaborately decorated—even with electric lights—about two weeks before Christmas. The mound of gifts under it, mostly wrapped in white or red tissue paper, grew from day to day as shopping expeditions were completed. We all gave a gift, no matter how small, to each family member. As children, we did most of our shopping in Woolworth's or Kresge's 5-and-10 cent stores. The gifts tended to be practical things that could be bought in this 5- and 10-cent range: a tube of toothpaste, a bar of shaving soap, new shoe laces, a handkerchief, a new comb, fingernail polish, an autograph book, colored pencils, a bag of marbles. All were purchased with our own money earned outside the home.

The cellar was a special, exciting and mysterious place in those weeks between Thanksgiving and Christmas because it was the scene of letters to Santa politely making our gift requests. They were deposited in the chimney clean-out iron door and instantly swept up in the draft. As we all very well knew, they were caught by one of Santa's brownies who lived in the chimney at this season, and thence delivered by him to Santa at the North Pole. We even received letters back from Santa on occasion, written in an almost indecipherable script. We carried on this correspondence with great care and some dread, since to allow a brownie to see you would negate the delivery of the letter. From time to time we spied the brown, pointed cap of one of these elves at the dining-room window, and were especially good following this experience. (The brownie, as we later learned, was Pa wearing a secret brown cap!)

On Christmas Eve the stockings of all believers were hung along the kitchen wall, beside the door, since we did not have a fireplace. Following this ceremony we three little kids—Phyllis, Betty and I—went off to our attic beds to await the morning. For the first hour or so we climbed into the same bed for mutual support and perhaps to spook each other. We were sure that we could hear the bells on Santa's sleigh and even the sound of reindeer on the roof, and thereafter quickly departed for our own beds so as to not be caught awake when the jolly old elf entered the kitchen.

Christmas morning was a wildly exciting maelstrom of emptying stockings of their toys, oranges, apples, and candy, combined with great relief that they did not contain lumps of coal signifying Santa's displeasure with some mis-deed of the past year. Toys I treasured the most were wind-up trains with tracks, and those multi-colored, whistling spinning tops. Later, we gathered around the tree for the gift exchange over which Pa presided, dressed in a Santa suit and beard. For several years, I really thought he *was* Santa! Everyone expressed surprise and many thanks for the gifts received. In those "pre-Hallmark" days, no Christmas cards were received or sent by mail and were not expected or missed; the day was a family household celebration.

New Year's Eve was not a celebration as such and was mostly recognized by bed-time remarks that, "I'll see you next year!" We devoted some time on New Year's Day itself to drawing up lists of resolutions to be observed in the coming year and these often had a moral deportment tone, such as, "I will not fight or argue," "I will never be late for school," "I will not grumble about doing my chores," and "I will not tease my sisters." These same good intentions were reiterated as the Lenten Season began, along with aspirations to give up candy, ice-cream or gum.

Easter, exclusive of the obligatory choir singing in the two morning services, was also the time to wear new finery—a new tie, shirts and shoes for the boys, and new bonnets, dresses, shoes and pocketbooks for the girls. Our Easter lily was displayed on a table in the living room. Hard-boiled eggs, dyed and hand-decorated with colored stripes, were eaten from egg cups on Easter morning. The children searched all corners and crannies of the house for hidden jelly beans. Usually we received an Easter basket filled with chocolate bunnies and marshmallow chickens in a nest of artificial grass. In the afternoon, we visited our brother John's grave and planted tulips there.

On Memorial Day we all wore red carnations to honor the living, or white ones in memory of the dead. We visited John's grave again and planted more flowers. Our large American flag was hung from the front porch eave and provided a translucent shade screen.

Whatever else it was supposed to be, the Fourth of July was fireworks in the back yard, purchased a day or two before from a stand near the Worcester Market: firecrackers, ladies' fingers, salutes, Roman candles, rockets, pin-wheels, fountains, sparklers. Firecrackers or salutes were fired off in the end of a length of waterpipe held by one of us and lit by another, with flames erupting from both ends. They were exploded under tin cans which rose high in the air unless the bottom blew out. On one occasion I became engrossed with these performances while holding a lit firecracker in my hand. The result was a badly burned hand and fingers which Ma coated with carbolic salve and wrapped in home-made bandages. In a few days it was completely healed. Roman candles, rockets, pin-wheels, fountains and sparklers were saved for after-dark displays. Once again, the flag hung at the front porch. Our own celebration was sufficient. We did not venture into the city for the parade and other ceremonies.

Preparation for Thanksgiving began in earnest a few days before this feast-day. Hubbard squashes, onions, turnips and apples were purchased from local farms to add to the carrots, beets and potatoes we grew ourselves. Three or four gallons of cider were bought at the cider mill. Bulk quantities of nuts—walnuts, Brazil nuts, filberts, almonds and pecans—as well as cranberries came from the barrels at Brockelman's Worcester Market. The twenty-pound (or more) turkey was selected from the specimens which hung by their feet from racks over the butcher's counter. The day before, the kitchen was a scene of hectic baking activity: apple, squash, pumpkin and mince pies, bread and "squash" biscuits by Ma and my sisters. Pa and the boys peeled potatoes, carrots and apples and kept the stove and oven hot.

One comical event which is still etched clearly in my memory, was the time I burst from the kitchen door and planted my right foot firmly in a fresh-baked squash pie which had been set there to cool. This is one of those things for which your family will always remember you at gatherings no matter what other great feats you may think you have accomplished!

Thanksgiving morning found Pearl supervising us as we cracked nuts and picked out the meats around the kitchen table while the turkey roasted in the oven. When Ma opened the door to baste it we were enveloped with its tantalizing aroma. At the same time, vegetables were boiling in their pots while cranberry sauce and gravy slowly simmered, and dumplings were cooked in gravy. Pa carved the bird as it lay in its great china plate on the kitchen table, providing slivers of meat to the "official taste-testers" who surrounded him. The potatoes and squash were vigorously mashed, mixed with butter and milk. The dining room table was covered with a heavy linen cloth with large matching napkins for us all. Boards were placed between some chairs with volumes of Dickens' books atop to seat the smaller children—Phyllis, Betty, Suzanne and me—between bigger people. Finally, the serving bowls were placed, the crystal glasses filled with ice water and cider, and Ma or Pa asked a Thanksgiving blessing, reminding us to think of those in greater need. The plates were passed and re-passed until we could eat no more. After a walk around the house or yard and a cleaning of the table, we returned to our bountiful board for slices of two or three varieties of pie, and handfuls of nuts washed down with cider or tea. The rest of the day was devoted to washing and drying dishes and a general clean-up of the kitchen. These gustatorial indulgences extended for many days as we feasted on the left-overs: turkey slices and dressing heated in gravy, hashes composed of a variety of mashed vegetables, the flavor of which seemed to improve with age, cranberry sauce, handfuls of cracked nuts with raisins, warmed up slices of pies, and finally spicy turkey soup!

Brother Fred's farm in Princeton was the scene of two memorable Thanksgivings. The house was a long rambling structure with several porches, and sheds that led into the barn. Great spreading maple trees along the road and in the yard were ablaze with autumnal colors. Ancient, lichen-encrusted stone walls bounded his property. The back yard pastures and orchards looked northward to Mount Wachusett projecting above the horizon. Fred kept horses, cows, goats, sheep, chickens and geese in addition to his full-time job. These creatures added an authentic touch to complete this traditional New England scene. (During two or three summer haying seasons I spent a day in his hay loft as he and my brothers pitched the hay up from the farm wagon. It was hard, sweaty, dusty work trying desperately to store those great clumps before they buried me in them!)

Birthdays were always recognized by a cake with the appropriate number of candles, and the singing of "Happy Birthday" around the supper table. Other than this, we did not make a great event of these milestones in our lives.

CHAPTER IV

Relatives, Neighbors, Visitors

Relatives

MY RECOLLECTION OF RELATIVES—aunts, uncles, cousins, nieces and nephews—are vague. For whatever reasons, we saw them infrequently, if at all, during my childhood. Many were only names referred to but not known. A few stand out clearly as "snapshots," despite my limited contact with them.

Suzanne, born in 1934, as the first child of brother Fred, lived with us for two years of her infancy and early childhood when Fred and Grace took up residence on the third floor of "552." She was a sweet, gentle child—more like another baby sister. I recall walking her around the kitchen floor, she standing on my toes as I held her by both hands—almost in a waltz step. In wintertime she would stand on the front of my skis for a glide down the backyard slope. We built snowmen together of big rolled snowballs with a broom stick for arms, lumps of coal for eyes, ears and mouth, sticks for a moustache and hair, and a crooked carrot for a nose. I walked her through the back yard and fields on sunny days of spring, summer and fall, pointing out flowers, trees and birds.

Uncle Fred Tracey, Ma's brother, was a tall, rough-hewn man, broad and sturdy of face and frame, with powerful hands reflecting his lifetime of physical toil. He was quiet and soft spoken, with a whimsical, enigmatic smile reminiscent of Abraham Lincoln's. After lighting his pipe, he and Ma would sit by the kitchen stove recalling their childhood days in MacPhee's Corner while we children listened quietly from our seats around the table. Our favorite tale, recounted over and over again, was of the time they met a bear on the path to their country school. Uncle Fred worked as a resident farmhand and groundskeeper at a convent in Shrewsbury, having moved, alone, to this area. Each summer he returned to MacPhee's Corner where his wife, Effie, and their two sons still lived. After an early supper he would "knock out" his pipe and climb aboard the bus again in order to retire early in anticipation of a workday which began at sunrise.

Ma's Uncle John Welch—the relative who I believe provided her with a home in Boston after she was orphaned—came to call on rare occasions. An immaculately dressed gentleman of small, spare stature and a swarthy, wizened complexion, his sparkling dark eyes reinforced his animated speech and personality. He was a waterfront missionary who went aboard ships distributing Bibles, spreading the word of God and offering a clean bed and hot meal ashore as well as encouraging the sailors' attendance at the chapel worship services. His conversation recounted some of his experiences in pursuit of his calling.

Angus MacPhee, Ma's cousin, lived in Shrewsbury where he was resident manager of a dairy farm and estate. He was an outgoing, gregarious man with a hearty, animated voice, ruddy complexion and powerful physique. On one or two occasions we visited at his home. His wife and daughter, Eileen (about my age), seemed to look with disdain at us. I felt uncomfortable in their presence, feeling that I should cover the patches or frayed knees of my knickers; even although they might have been relatively new at the time! I wish I could have known Angus better. To me, he was the epitome of what an uncle ought to be.

I presume Laura MacPhee, Ma's registered nurse cousin, was Angus' sister. She lived in Oxford. I don't recall ever seeing her, although I suppose she may have called on us at some time.

Gladys Miller and her husband—a brother of James Miller of MacPhee's Corner, Nova Scotia, who was married to Ma's sister Eunice—also lived in Shrewsbury. She was another of Ma's cousins—a most gracious, soft-spoken lady with whom we would have tea at their home or ours on all too infrequent occasions.

Uncle John Kemp, Pa's brother, and his wife, Myrtie, lived on the shore of Lake Quinsigamond in Worcester where they had extensive vegetable and flower gardens. He was a quiet, reflective man of small but wiry stature and looked quite a bit like Pa. I always enjoyed their brief visits. They had two sons, Arthur and Howard, our cousins.

Howard Kemp was about brother Fred's age and shared some of his interests in automobiles and motorcycles. At one time they both owned 1930 Packard convertible coupes as well as Harley-Davidson motorcycles. I was in awe of, and somewhat terrified by, these vehicles as their engines were tuned up in our driveway or in the barn.

Arthur Kemp, Howard's younger brother, was of a more serious nature. He went on to a managerial position in one of the utility companies of Worcester and also earned quite a reputation as a golfer. Both were possessed of powerful physiques, glowing good health and outgoing, warm personalities.

I have vague recollections of Aunt Ada, Pa's older sister, and the probable source of "Aunt Eva's tea" served to the children. A diminutive, gentle, smiling lady with an artistic demeanor, she and her husband lived on Gates Lane, a country road in the rural west end of Worcester. I remember that they kept numerous cats, both inside and outside of their house. The old cider mill was nearby, giving us another reason to visit them in the fall.

Every three or four years on unpredictable days of early summer or fall, sister Eva and her husband, Joe Richards, would sweep unannounced into our driveway in their latest new black Buick, from their home in central Ohio. I met Eva briefly only five or six times in my entire life from childhood to adulthood and so perceived her as a distant relative—perhaps an aunt—rather than as a sister. Joe had been a Methodist minister in several small Ohio towns, but subsequently left the ministry to go into the laundromat business. It was rumored that he was also quite successful with stock market investments. After some obligatory small talk over tea, Joe might be moved to contribute to our cultural enrichment with a self-accompanied, slightly off-key solo rendition of "The Holy City" at Olive's piano. Brother Dick sang it better; Olive played it better. In less than an hour they would make their departure for appointments with "very important people" in Framingham, Boston or Cambridge, to be followed, as they put it, by Joe's annual "bear-hunting" trip and visit to the horse-race tracks of New Hampshire.

Neighbors

The neighbors who lived in close proximity to us would be called our "extended family" in today's sociological jargon. These were the families with whom we shared, to a greater or lesser degree, the experiences of life in the 1920's and 1930's. The children of these families were our most frequent playmates. We knew about many of the happy or sad events in each others' lives, shared thoughts, dreams, plans, worries—even though we seldom entered each others' homes. Home in those days was the family castle, reserved for relatives and occasional formal visitors. Mothers borrowed small cooking items from each other by sending a child next door, perhaps for a cup of sugar or flour, an egg or seasonings, which were always returned in a day or two. Kids of the neighborhood called others to play by standing outside of back doors, the call being delivered in a sing-song voice while assuming a ceremonial posture. If there was no response we left and never presumed to knock at the door or even worse, use the telephone for this frivolous purpose. Parents were addressed formally and politely as "Mr." or "Mrs.," and they in turn addressed us by our first names as the children we were.

Men always wore felt hats out-of-doors—well "broken-in" models for every day and yard work. They normally wore neckties as well, even with work clothes—which were usually just "best clothes" that had seen better days. Until they reached teenage years, boys wore knee-length "knickers" with long stockings. The day of specialized leisure and/or work clothes had not yet arrived. Women and girls always wore dresses or skirts; it was unheard of for them to wear slacks or shorts. They also wore a hat of some kind on almost every occasion, and always in church.

Ward and Helen Pratt lived across the street with their children, Arnold, who was Dick's age, and Priscilla, who was a year older than me but acted at least five years older! Their white veranda'd house and barn sat on a hillside with a steep driveway. Mr. Pratt took the bus every morning to his office job with the Grattin-Knight Leather Tanning Company—often with a predictable comment to the driver and other passengers, that this was "a rough-riding bus on two shredded wheat biscuits for breakfast!"

Mrs. Pratt gave elocution lessons in her living room. She always dressed formally, with pince-nez spectacles hung by a silver chain around her neck when they were not perched on her nose. They spent two weeks every summer at a vacation lodge on the shores of Wells Beach, Maine, traveling in their four-door, tan Model A Ford.

The Almgrens, with their son Herbert (Charlie's age) and daughters Helen (my age) and Ruth (Betty's age), lived next door to the north. Mrs. Almgren was justifiably proud of her excellent Swedish cooking—especially her pastries. Mr. Almgren kept chickens in a coop behind their house, near their vegetable gardens. We often watched from the dining room window as he mowed his lawn in gradually decreasing circles until he reached the oak tree which grew at the center. This exercise always reminded me of someone winding a gigantic watch spring!

The Lindbergs lived to the south, just beyond our cornfield. They also had a barn, vegetable gardens, chickens, and several goats as well. Mr. Lindberg was reputed to make elderberry wine. They had two daughters—Ruth, my age, and Margerie, Betty's age.

Freelands' house and barn was on the high hill behind Pratts', reached by a long, winding driveway. They kept horses and did some part-time farming. They had several children as well. Fordyce was Dick's age; Marion was my age.

The Halpins, quiet, hard-working folks, lived just beyond Freelands' driveway in a tidy brown house with a matching barn. Mr. Halpin was the caretaker of the large Alton estate bordering his property. Further still down Chandler Street where it met May Street, lived Mr. and Mrs. Dorr with their daughter and her two children. Charlie Dorr was a spry, bow-legged leprechaun of cheerful demeanor. He was the caretaker of the old Lincoln farm and estate across the street. They lived in an authentic, quaint Cape Cod cottage which sat on a knoll. It was one of the oldest houses in Worcester. They still used kerosene lamps and candles, heated their home with wood stoves and fireplaces and got their water from a hand pump at the kitchen sink. A working spinning wheel stood in the corner. A visit to their home was like a magical trip back to the "olden days."

After our cornfield was sold, the two houses built there were occupied by the Sandersons and their two sons, Roger and Walter; and the Roses, who had a daughter, Virginia, and two sons, Stuart and Donald.

Visitors

Many of these visitors were sad, lonely people who, because of Ma and Pa, probably viewed our house as a temporary refuge—a place to call home if only for an hour or two, or a day or two. The memory of some of these has already faded.

The first warm, sunny days of June often heralded the arrival of John Dana. He pushed rather than rode his rickety old bicycle which was laden with all sorts of bundles. He often had a small wagon in tow as well which was piled high variously with chairs, dishes, pots and pans, books, curtains and drapes, cardboard boxes and other "necessaries" which he had collected during the winter. John would be on his way to his Leicester "estate," about ten miles from our house, and perhaps fourteen miles from his rooms in downtown Worcester. He would stop in for mid-morning tea and toast, and some pleasant conversation with Ma and Pa or others who happened to be at home. Even though his clothes were rumpled, he always wore a shirt and tie, suitcoat or blazer, and a felt or straw hat. John spoke impeccable English in a well-modulated voice, and was quite elegant in manner. With little or no prompting, he would spontaneously recite lines of poetry, usually of the English Romantic Period— by Wordsworth, Lord Byron, Shelley—or Bobby Burns, and shortly thereafter be off to the hills again. He was always received warmly to our kitchen or porches. I later discovered the destination of his treasures; his "estate" was an open field with heaps of clothes, dishes, lumber, furniture and other articles scattered about. John could often be found seated under a tree reading, enjoying the view or receiving visitors.

On summer days, usually at noon-time and just before "dinner-time," we could also expect either "The Deaf Man" or "Aunt Hattie" to come calling. The Deaf Man—I never knew his name or where he lived—was a tall, raw-boned, heavy-jawed man who always announced his presence with a loud knock at the front door. Even in the heat of mid-summer he wore a wool tweed suit coat and pants, wool shirt and tie, long underwear, heavy ankle-length leather shoes and a wide-visored cap which was placed on the top of the hall bookcase, covering his cigarettes. He seemed a bit addled, I suppose because of his deafness. He talked in a booming drawl and we in turn, had to "speak up" in order to be heard by him. The talk always turned to farming and farms he knew to be for sale. I suppose he was a real estate broker of sorts; Ma and Pa sometimes investigated these properties after his departure. He took his leave politely after an hour or so, thanking Ma for the dinner.

Aunt Hattie, the oldest sister of Grace—Fred's wife—also could be expected to arrive unexpectedly someday about noon, having walked all the way from her family farm in Hubbardston, some ten or twelve miles to the north. She carried her cardboard suitcase under her arm prepared to spend three or four days with us. She was a big, strong, heavy-set woman, dressed in a wool coat, heavy leather walking shoes and plain homespun dresses. Although she talked but little, she often baked pies, cakes, bread and cookies for us and generally helped out around the house. As she arrived, so she would depart one morning with no previous indication of this intent.

Three of my favorite visitors for tea, toast and conversation were Jimmy Spellman, Wayne Woodis and Jonny Farr. All three were gregarious, vigorous and handsome young men in their mid to late twenties. Wayne had been a close friend of our brother John, as had been Jimmy. Jonny Farr had been one of Eva's boyfriends. Despite the fact that their primary connections to our family had been dissolved, they maintained contact with us for years thereafter. Wayne died of spinal meningitis before he reached thirty years, and Jimmy died in his early thirties, making a triple tragedy with brother John's death at nineteen, of peritonitis following his appendectomy. It seems plausible that all three of these deaths would have been prevented by the sulfanilamide or antibiotics of modern medical practice.

CHAPTER V

Fun and Frolics: High-Jinx and Mischief

Kids at Play

IN SPRING, SUMMER OR FALL when daylight—or at least dusk—lasted until nine o'clock, the boys and girls of the neighborhood would gather after supper, usually in our yard, to play those old timeless games: tag, hide-and-go-seek, sixty-outs, red-rover, red-light, kick-the-can, leap-frog. One way or another we engaged in the more organized sports as well: baseball with one or more bases—both the ball and bat being held together with friction tape—and tag football under the street light in front of Pratts' house. Our "football" was a five-pound cloth sugar bag stuffed with leaves or grass. Our tennis practice court was a brick wall behind the Normal School. We played horseshoes with real horseshoes from horses' hooves and lengths of iron water pipe for the goals.

Priscilla Pratt wrote and directed several one-act plays, the most memorable of which was *The Grasshopper and the Ant*, performed in our back field. I was cast in the role of the carefree, happy-go-lucky grasshopper, clad in green shirt, pants and hat, who took no thought for the morrow and was thereby destined to beg for food and shelter from the prudent ant when the frigid frosts and blizzards of winter descended. Phyllis, I recall, was the serious, sober, hard-working ant dressed in black who laid away provisions during the days of summer and fall. The props for this comedy/tragedy included a three-foot high gravel ant hill into which the ant could disappear. Although we had a ticket office, we were unsuccessful in attracting any paying customers—but nevertheless, the show went on!

I had acquired a lop-sided, discarded football as a result of my attending gridiron contests at Worcester Polytechnic Institute where Pa was now groundskeeper. Having watched many spectacular kick-offs, punts and field goals, I was confident I could duplicate those prodigious feats with a place-kick from our side yard clear over the house and into Almgren's yard. As soon as the ball left my toe, it went into agonizing slow motion, and I knew its altered pre-ordained destination was one of the large window panes of the living room. I was right. It passed slowly through the window with a prolonged "K-e-r-ra-s-h!!," showering shards of glass on Olive's piano keyboard. Immediately thereafter, football was declared off limits in any part of the yard.

In springtime we practiced the lost art of swinging birches. This was an awesome challenge: to pick a tree that was high enough but not too high, and that grew at a sufficient angle so that we could shinny up the outside curve to just the right height. Then, grasping the trunk with both hands, we flung ourselves off into space for an exhilarating arc-shaped descent to the ground. If we jumped too soon we were suspended in mid-air, perhaps ten or fifteen feet up, with the only recourse being a drop to the ground. One of these mis-judgments led to my broken arm, initially reported to Ma as, "I think my arm is a little bent."

Emulating Tarzan of radio and movie fame, we also had a grape-vine swing which hung from an oak tree growing on The Island, just at the edge of the pond. By grasping the vine at a mad dash we could swing far out from shore and drop into the water, thereby escaping from African warriors with long spears, or charging lions, tigers, or rhinoceroses, only to be beset by the imaginary huge, ravenous crocodiles who lurked in these shallows with toothed jaws agape as they lashed their spiny tails.

The drone of an airplane overhead would result in kids and parents bolting from their doors with the cry, "*Airplane! Airplane!*" while craning their necks to see this rare marvel in the sky. Dick, who as a teen-ager was obsessed with dime novels and movies depicting American and German dog-fights between Spads and Fokkers over the battlefields of World War I, would resolve once again to learn to fly some day. He eventually did so.

On warm, clear nights of August, sister Pearl or Gladys might lead Phyllis, Betty and me to the open fields of the Lincoln Farm, there to lie on our backs to watch shooting stars and to trace constellations in the dark sky: the Big Dipper, the North Star, Orion, Cassiopeia, Pegasus, and on particularly clear nights, even Draco the Dragon and the Pleiades.

Winter Sports

The winter skating season was preceded by "rubber ice" running when the ice was perhaps only a quarter-inch thick. This technique required a dash across a frozen shallow cove, swamp, or even the farm cesspool. If you were fast enough, your feet left cob-web shaped indentations in the ice. If you were too slow you fell through, leaving you with yet another explanation to Ma of how this misfortune occurred. When the pond was safely frozen but still clear of snow, we brothers and sisters along with many neighborhood kids could be found skating, mostly with those clamp-on skates that could be attached to our shoe soles. They inflicted excruciating pain on our ankles. Our snap-the-whip chains often had ten or more "links." We admired the figure-skating of Mr. and Mrs. Erickson and Mr. and Mrs. Sundholm who performed in the cove bordering their home. From time to time we skated at night around a ceremonial bonfire, gazed at the bright stars overhead, and listened with consternation to the ice growl and thump as it contracted or expanded, creating ominous, deep cracks which caught our skate blades.

Toward the end of February when the ice had frozen to a thickness of two feet or so, the annual ice-harvesting operation of the Torpey Ice Company commenced. A crew of sturdy men dressed in heavy wool mackinaws, wool caps, scarves and mittens and shod with overshoes or hunting boots, cut blocks of ice by hand with long rough-toothed saws after an initial cut had been made with an axe. They pushed the blocks along an ever-lengthening channel toward the ice-house, using peaveys—long-handled tools with heavy iron hooks at one end. A horse-powered moving escalator carried the blocks up into the ice-house at a very steep angle, shoved along by more men with peaveys. Sawdust was packed around the ice for insulation. We watched this activity with great excitement, skating as close to the open water as we dared until we were chased off by one of the men. (Patch's Pond, as well as Mill Pond and Coes Pond had been created by damming up different segments of the same brook, primarily to produce ice in the winter, although water-

Skaters and Ice Harvesters on Patch's Pond

wheels at the dams were also used to power mills of one kind or another.)

Torpey's Ice House burned to the ground one August night. This spectacular fire-storm lit up the western horizon as giant tongues of flame and great showers of sparks rose high in the sky. It was officially reported that spontaneous combustion of the damp sawdust had caused this conflagration. Another opinion held that it had been set off by some tough guys just for the excitement of watching the fire trucks arrive in a vain attempt to extinguish this inferno.

When sufficient snow had accumulated, we pulled our sleds through the woods and over the steep hill behind Freelands' for about a half-mile until we arrived at Brantwood Road, a steep, paved road with street lights which was reserved for sliding in the evenings, with no cars allowed.

By any measure the longest, most exciting and challenging sled run was down the steep, mountainous road leading to the top of Torpey's Hill, now the end of one of the Worcester Airport runways. There was little or no danger of meeting automobiles or trucks since this grade was usually impassable in the winter. The only house on it was that of our iceman, Ben Mountain, about half-way up. He and his family used horse and wagon transportation, or walked. The climb of a mile or more while pulling our sled was tiring, especially if we made two or three runs, but it was well worth the effort. My brothers recounted even more exhilarating wild, reckless descents down this grade than I experienced on my sled. They rode on a six-man "double-runner" bob-sled owned by one of their friends.

In daylight hours we slid on Hartshorn Hill which is now covered with a hundred or more houses where woods and hay-fields had been. It was here at about the age of nine that I hit a tree while rounding a sharp, banked curve. When I "came to," lying on my sled and dripping blood, I was being pulled home by Phyllis. She thought I was dead. My upper lip still carries the scar of this misadventure.

The best tobogganing was from the top of Freelands' hill through several Lake Placid-type bobsled turns and over a fifteen-foot embankment where we were airborne until we alighted on Chandler Street. This called for one of us to be guard and signal when no cars were coming. The curved front of our toboggan was replaced by sheet metal after we hit a tree on one memorable run.

Skiing on the hill behind the Normal School called for making two straight tracks and a modest jump. We were on long wooden skis waxed with an old candle with only a leather toe-

Moonlight Ski at the Reservoir

strap for bindings. Our ski poles were saplings cut from the woods.

My fondest skiing memory from those days is of a moonlight trek with Dick down an old logging road leading to the Tatnuck Reservoirs. It was a very cold, clear night; if we stood still for a moment not a sound could be heard except our own breathing. The snow whistled and squeaked as we passed over it and the powder thrown up at turns glistened in the eerie light of the moon. Gliding to a stop, we gazed across the wide, trackless expanse of the frozen reservoir to the snow-capped pines on the far shore, and listened to the silence once again.

Railroad Trains

Arnold Pratt had a life-long romance with railroads beginning at an early age, particularly steam locomotives and the crack passenger and freight trains which they pulled. This early interest eventually led to a life-long career working for the Soo Line. He knew the name, number and ownership of every significant locomotive and train nation-wide. His room looked like a railroad ticket agent's office, with rack on rack of timetables, and walls covered with pictures of famous "iron horses." He knew the exact time to the minute when a train was due at a given crossing or station within a radius of twenty-five or more miles of our neighborhood. His father would sometimes drive us to a particular rendezvous in his 1930 Model A Ford just to watch these monsters roar through remote crossings, their piercing, shrieking whistles striking terror in our hearts as they approached. The whirlwind aftermath sucked at our knees as they thundered past with drive wheels pumping furiously. The engineer, eyes encased in smoked-glass goggles, a red bandanna around his neck and his visored striped cap pulled down, waved from his cab, followed by the trainman's salute from the caboose. As a grand finale, we were enveloped in the clouds of hot steam, smoke and cinders which marked their passage. We visited stations where freight, mail and passengers were unloaded just to assure they were on time to the minute. They always were. Memorabilia from these excursions took the form of pennies which had been placed on the tracks, now expanded to the size of quarters!

On another occasion, Charlie and Dick experienced a terrifying descent down Belmont Hill in Pa's truck while helping him on the milk delivery route. This steep grade ended at the Lincoln Square railroad crossing. The truck brakes failed just as the crossing gates closed with warning bells and lights signalling the approach of a long freight train. By shifting down to first gear and finally forcing his lever into reverse, Pa finally brought the careening wagon to a shuttering, lurching halt while milk bottles and cases tumbled about. They stopped just short of the gate as the locomotive lumbered past. After a moment or two, they regained sufficient composure to allow a count of the number of cars in the train—well over one hundred!

High-Jinx and Mischief

One of the favorite summer evening pastimes of Dick, Charlie, Arnold Pratt and Fordie Freeland which I was allowed to join was the singing of old-time songs under the cedar trees on Pratts' lawn. Dick accompanied all of them with the four chords he had mastered on his second-hand ukulele. We knew all verses of twenty or more of those oldies which can still be found in music volumes dedicated to this high purpose. We sang raucously and lustily to the amusement and sometimes annoyance of parents and other adults. Some of these numbers can no longer be found in published form and thus may have passed into "oral history," e.g.: "My Pal Was A Fair-Square Young Puncher," "When The Work's All Done This Fall," "The Run-away Train," "The Letter Edged In Black," "Silver-Haired Daddy of Mine," "Wizard Oil" and other radio commercials. Fred joined us once or twice to sing his all-time, life-time favorite—"The Long, Long Trail."

Although we were entirely oblivious to this circumstance at the time, it now appears that our song-fests under Pratts' cedars coincided closely with the founding of *The Society for the Preservation and Encouragement of Barbershop Quartet Singing in America* in 1938—in Tulsa, Oklahoma. Both groups were dedicated to the same high purpose of singing the good old songs!

On other evenings this same group would gather in the brush at the top of the Chandler Street bluff to play the disappearing box trick on passing motorists. A large, attractively wrapped box was placed on the side of the road with a length of clothesline attached to it, leading to our hideaway. Cars would slow down, then stop and back up to retrieve this package. Meanwhile we had pulled it up, hiding it and ourselves. They backed up well beyond us, searching in vain. Occasionally they would drive back and forth several times before departing. This mischief came to an end one evening when an unmarked police car stopped, disgorging four large men in blue. They chased us unsuccessfully through the fields and woods, but kept our box and rope.

During the construction of two new houses on the site of our former cornfield, the two old-time Swedish carpenters built a sturdy shack, complete with a door, two windows, a shingled roof and a wood-stove with its pipe rising through the roof. They ate their lunch here during cold days of winter. We were not allowed into their inner sanctum although we often enjoyed it after they left for the day by climbing through a window since the door was padlocked. One cold winter noon, in the interest of seeing what would happen, Charlie and Dick crept behind the shed and up onto the roof, placing a board over the smoking stovepipe and quickly departing to watch the consequences at a safe distance, joined by several of us "observers." After a few minutes of adjusting the dampers, the two carpenters burst from the door followed by a dense cloud of smoke. They cussed us out soundly in Swedish as well as English. We couldn't blame them when they told Ma about this incident. They were really good men who often talked to us, showed us some techniques of carpentry—they worked exclusively with hand tools—and let us collect scrap wood for kindling, and "not-so-scrap" boards to build our own shack and other artifacts.

Two of Pa's old Dodge milk trucks, which for one reason or another could no longer be driven on the road, were parked in the back woods. Charlie and Dick were able to get them started with a hand crank since they had no batteries. I suspect they also may have siphoned gasoline from Pa's car. Used motor oil was free from the Socony station crankcase drainings. So equipped, they learned to drive in the fields and woods. They also became "race car drivers" around an improvised dirt track. The trucks became a special mode of transportation to The Point for swimming, often with three or four kids riding the running boards. On one occasion I spun off into the woods at a sharp turn, having lost my grip. On another, one of the Dodges finally came to rest in about three feet of water, having lost all braking power. It took a small army of kids to push, pull or otherwise roll it back onto the shore. Piece by piece the trucks lost their doors, windows, seats, roof, mufflers, tires, and brakes, but could still run on their steel rims. Eventually they were sold for scrap metal.

Charlie and Dick owned similar cars by the time they were in their late teens. Charlie's was a tan 1932 Plymouth convertible coupe with a rumble seat, Dick's a blue 1933 Plymouth coupe. With these advanced models, their racing exploits escalated to the half-mile straight-away down Chandler Street to May Street. On one occasion, the course started north of the blind corner with a collaborator signalling, "all clear—no cars coming." They came around the bend neck-and-neck, blocking both lanes of the pavement. These contests were scheduled when Ma and Pa were away shopping at the Worcester Market, or perhaps examining another farm in the country. However, the word got out to Ma and Pa, and the police department patrols as well, so these speedway events came to a halt.

Two old pairs of well-worn, scuffed boxing gloves hung in the cellarway. I think Freddie owned them. This was during the era of Joe Louis' ascendancy to the heavyweight championship of the world. Charlie and Dick set up a ring of sorts where the barn once stood, and there contended with themselves as well as other stalwarts of their age for the Chandler Street/Tatnuck Square title. These matches were permanently canceled the day that Charlie knocked Dick cold with a left to the solar plexus and a right cross to the temple. After a count of twenty seconds or less which felt like an hour, the alarm was raised, bringing Ma running in panic with a pail of cold water. Dick was revived, the boxing gloves disappeared—probably by Pa's hand—and the arena was converted to a flower garden.

When Dick was about sixteen he came home with a brand-new single-shot 12-gauge shotgun for which he had been saving his money. It was a beauty with its iridescent blued metal parts and a highly polished walnut stock. He became quite proficient at shooting squirrels, rabbits and pheasants. Even so, he occasionally felt the need for target practice while standing in the back yard by scattering the flocks of pigeons which alighted in our corn fields. One day he went too far in the view of Ma, and the consternation and strong objections of the neighbors who were uncomfortably close to the trajectory of some of his pellets. It seems that he had decided to test his skill with high-angle shots from the attic windows by shooting at the crows on Chandler Street. Shooting was limited to fields and woods a safe distance from houses thereafter.

One of our paths led through the back woods and fields around the Lincoln Farm cesspool to the pigsty behind the barn.

It was still occupied by a dozen or so porkers. Charlie and Dick and others of us as well, would, on occasion, harass the poor creatures with tossed sticks or stones just to hear them squeal. These excursions might continue with an exploration of the cavernous barn, entered through a gloomy, damp, cellar passageway hung with cobweb shrouds. Old farm wagons and equipment, long silent, stood on the main floor between the empty horse stalls. The hay loft still held mountains of hay.

From there we continued into the mansion house itself via an unlocked window on the back porch; we called it the haunted house. We wandered through the spacious kitchen and pantry, the panelled dining room and library, the ballroom-sized parlor and on up the bannistered staircase to the king-sized bedrooms. Although empty of furniture, it still imparted a sense of its story-book life of bygone days.

Boys of eleven or twelve can be insufferably "nosey" and real pains in the neck to older siblings, and I was no exception. I was unbearably curious as to what Dick and Arnold Pratt were up to when they disappeared up the ladder leading to Pratts' barn hayloft, from which I was excluded. They finally told me they were playing cards—"Penny Poker," whatever that was. They were joined by "Betsy" now and then in another version called "Strip Poker." (Her real name escapes me, although I never thought that could be, since I was secretly, madly in love with her—even though she never acknowledged my existence by so much as a wave or a "hi"! She was probably about fifteen or sixteen and had long, shiny black hair and sparkling dark eyes.) She took advanced "elocution" lessons from Mrs. Pratt, following which she waited in their yard for her father to pick her up at the end of his work day. I finally was given a part to play in this scenario after being sworn to secrecy. My role was to hang around the barn door, pretending to help put away tools while keeping an eye out for Mrs. Pratt or Ma, should they appear in the yard. In this event, I was to whistle "Red River Valley" while rattling the barn door, giving the poker players time to hide the evidence.

Smoking holds a fascination for kids as they approach their teen-age years and respond to the yearning to be "grown-up," and it did for us back then. After all, Uncle Fred always smoked a pipe as did Mr. Halpin and Ben Mountain, and the legendary Santa Claus as well. My experiments with this medium took the form of dry corn silk stuffed into a bowl carved from a "horse cobbler" nut or a very large acorn, with a hollow milkweed stalk as the stem. This folklore was passed from boy to boy, I suppose from time immemorial. Having succeeded in reducing the tongue of flame erupting from my bowl to a bed of coals, I set about to enjoy this forbidden pleasure. I did not find it to be pleasant at all. It burned my tongue and watered my eyes and so I quit the practice.

In the days before "trick or treat," rag-shag parades and neighborhood or town Halloween parties, we carved grotesque faces into real pumpkins, lit them with candles and placed them in our front windows, safe from marauding goblins and other spooks. We also stood in the back yard after dark looking for witches that might fly across the harvest moon.

Beginning in my twelfth year and continuing into early teen-age years, Halloween was also an evening for running wild after supper, at least for my friends and me, and probably for my brothers. Included were activities that I'm sure Ma and Pa never knew of or suspected. As is practiced today by many kids, vague, evasive answers were given to parents' inquiries when you were up to no good; e.g.:—"Where are you going?"—"Just out to play" or, "Just taking a walk to Tatnuck Square for an ice cream cone" or, "Going to look at the moon or the carved pumpkins along the street." "Who are you going with?"—"Some kids from school." "I want you home by nine o'clock." —"OK." Then later that evening: "What did you do?"—"Nothing much; guess I'll go to bed now."

The truth was that I was one of a gang of boys who ran howling through yards tipping garbage cans, cutting clothes-lines, taking down picket fences. We wore our oldest clothes and blackened our faces with burnt cork as a disguise. Rotten fruit was thrown against houses, windows were soaped or waxed, carved pumpkins were smashed in the street, roads were blocked with logs or boxes. Our grand finale was to pull the trolleys off the power line of trolley cars at Tatnuck Square by pulling the rope which raised or lowered the power rod. We harassed cars coming from the city as well as those trying to return to it. An awesome but harmless shower of blue and white sparks was produced as the trolley rod touched the power line. This cut off all power to the car and required the conductor to alight and walk to the back of the car to replace the wheel on the power line. As soon as he returned to his controls and got under way one of us yahoos would pull it off again. In this way we stranded five or six cars until we were dispersed by the arrival of several police cruisers.

Along The Waterfront

Most boys like to build things. Many of our constructions were devices to be enjoyed at or near the pond. We built camps out of scrap lumber held together with rusty bent nails. Old planks could be shaped into boats—the seams "waterproofed" with old rags and tar—and propelled by home-made paddles. Canoes could be fashioned from saplings for the frame and ribs, and dis-carded canvas as the shell. Judiciously placed rocks were used to give them the proper trim.

One winter, Dick labored hard and long in the cellar build-ing an advanced model canoe from which he could fish for bass in the coming spring. Its canvas skin was painted dark green; it looked like an Old Town model pictured in the L. L. Bean catalog. We launched it for its maiden voyage on Patch's Pond one cold March day, just after "ice-out." Shortly after we left the shore one of the "balance" boulders shifted violently and exited through a weak seam in the bottom of the craft. Needless to say, it quickly filled with ice water and sank, carried to its final rest-ing place by the several rocks we had installed. After flailing our way to shore we built a fire; we had taken the precaution of leav-ing some emergency matches on dry land. After reaching a rela-tively dry and warm state, we headed for home, beating it up to our rooms to change our clothes. Ma was too busy with other matters to notice our rumpled, damp condition. The canoe, I'm sure, still rests on the bottom of Patch's, now covered with close to sixty years' accumulation of mud and leaves. Perhaps, some centuries from now, an archaeologist will discover it, attributing its construction to primitive peoples who once lived on the shores of this pond!

We also built iceboats, made from 2x4's with old clamp skates for runners; an old sheet or blanket for a sail, kayaks (a plank held afloat with two three-gallon oil cans), rafts, and diving boards. My favorite artifacts were stilts made from 2x4's with a block to hold our feet three or four feet off the ground. We walked all the way to the pond on them and sometimes across the cove, at least until one stuck in the mud, catapulting you into the water. We made slingshots from a tree crotch and sections of old inner tubes, bow and arrows from saplings with chicken feathers as arrow stabilizers, and telephones of tin cans connected with lengths of wire, which worked marvelously in our imagination.

The Point, that finger of land extending into Patch's Pond with its stands of tall pines, was the focal point of our summer-time pleasures. We spent countless hours there, sometimes the whole day. It was our private summer camp during those years when summer camps of the YMCA or other organizations were unknown to us. We often ate our noontime meal in the shade of the pine grove. We roasted corn and potatoes in the hot coals of our fireplace. Sometimes we grilled hot dogs on a stick, garnished with our own tomatoes and cucumbers.

We all learned to swim at The Point, held up under our bellies by older brothers and sisters; first, floating, then the dog-paddle, and progressively the side-stroke, breast-stroke, back-stroke, under-water, and finally, the crawl! We became proficient at holding our breath under water for one to two minutes, and learned the rudiments of diving—cannon-balls, jack-knives, swan dives—from diving boards we made ourselves. Success was achieved when you could swim across The Point to the other side, about one hundred feet—even under water! The ultimate goals were to swim to The Island—about one thousand feet, then to the dam—about fifteen hundred feet—and finally to either the Mill Street shore or the ice house, each about a half-mile, initially accompanied by an older sibling to save you from drowning. The Ice House goal was considerably more risky, since the MacGoon family who lived near it was rumored to take pot shots with their 22's at those who approached too near to their territory! On one occasion while I was swimming with Dick, we heard the "crack-crack" of their firings followed by the

Swimming at The Point

"zing-zap" of the bullets over our heads. We quickly reversed our course, swam under water until out of breath, and went into a fast crawl back to The Point.

Stone-skipping contests were held on these shores, calling for long, patient searches for flat stones of just the right shape and size. Claims of ten to fifteen skips were not unusual.

We fished the coves for perch, bass and hornpout. Our tackle was handmade; a sapling from the woods, any available string, bottle corks for floats, a single hook baited with worms or night crawlers dug from our garden. Neighbors with shore-front property often lent us their rowboats to aid us in our quest. Ma frequently cooked our catch for supper, fried in Crisco, in her iron skillet. No outboard motors or other power boats ever disturbed the peace and quiet of this pond throughout the years of my childhood.

The Point also served as our out-of-doors bathtub on many summer days, particularly after completing some dusty, dirty, sweaty work in the yard or gardens. We lathered up from head to toe with our bar of Ivory soap while standing in the shallow water along the shore. An underwater swim rinsed away the suds, followed by a brisk toweling. Sometimes we just stretched out on the diving board or raft until the hot rays of the sun dried us off. This was an infinitely more pleasurable way to satisfy Ma's credo that "cleanliness is next to Godliness" than sitting in the bathtub at home when some member of the family might have an urgent need to use the bathroom facilities just as you got all soaped up!

Day-Trips and Other Special Outings

The days of July and early August heralded the blueberry season. Our whole family would gather all available pails, pans and pots and head for a day in the pastures of Hubbardston, or sometimes Torpey's Hill, to harvest this bounty. We gathered them by the gallon, observed occasionally by a curious cow or bull whose domains we had invaded. We ate our lunch of sandwiches washed down with home-made lemonade in the shade of pasture pine trees. The two most feared disasters were to spill an almost-full container into the tall grass, or to have inadvertently picked several "stink bugs" which could spoil the taste of your berries. These were great fun days—competing for the best bush, the most or the bluest, or the sweetest berries. Berries not consumed for our own needs were boxed and sold on our farm stand in front of the house.

When automobiles were available one way or another, Pa would drive a carload of us, after supper, to the Rutland Band Concerts, held on Wednesday evenings of summer. It was a journey of fifteen miles or so, up Route 122 through West Tatnuck, past Muir's Laundry Farm with lettering on the barn roof proclaiming, "We Soak The Clothes, Not the Customers," by the Paxton Steamer (an ice-cream, popcorn and hot dog emporium in the shape of a ferry boat on the bank of a small pond), across the Ware River bridge and on to the high country of Rutland with its band-stand on the town common. Brass bands from many towns, and even cities, performed here. As each musical selection began, all children of age twelve and under ran round-and-round the bandstand like an animated carousel. When the music stopped, they stopped as the horns of cars parked around the common sounded their appreciation. Usually we were treated to a five-cent ice cream cone or popcorn from Jack's Stand before departing for "552."

Even in the depths of the Depression, Ma and Pa would on occasion take in a double-feature movie with two or three of us small fry in tow. They favored the Plymouth Theater on Main Street, next to Mechanics Hall—famous in its own right for boxing matches, wrestling, roller-derbies and marathon dances. The Plymouth, while lacking the grandiose splendor of The Palace or The Capitol theaters with their rococo ornamentation and chandeliers, and four-manual pipe-organ concerts as well, offered what we enjoyed at half the price—a quarter for adults, accompanied kids free. Typical programs would open with *The Pathe News* "The Eyes And Ears Of The World," followed by a

Mickey Mouse or Looney-Tunes cartoon. The first feature film might be a cowboy and Indians saga starring Tom Mix, or possibly a slap-stick comedy by Charlie Chaplin, Laurel and Hardy or W. C. Fields. The second feature was usually of the romantic genre as performed by Rudolph Valentino or Douglas Fairbanks and their leading ladies of the day. John Boles was Ma's favorite leading man. *Previews of Coming Attractions* wound things up for the night. I am sure that these rare evenings at the movies were one of the few ways in which Ma and Pa could lay aside for a time their constant worries about providing food, shelter and clothing to their brood.

A Day At The Beach

During the Depression, the lack of a family automobile in good running order did not stop us from enjoying an annual summer day on the ocean beaches of New Hampshire or southern Maine. On these occasions, Pa would visit Bland's Dodge and Plymouth Dealership on Park Avenue and arrange for a free weekend "trial" of a second-hand car, implying he might consider buying one. I surmise he had in more prosperous years bought his milk trucks there and so had a "leg-up" in this transaction. However, I doubt if Mr. Bland was aware that this trial would include a round-trip drive of 150 miles or more. (Pa did eventually buy another car from him in 1936, a 1932 blue, four-door Plymouth, which turned out to be his last car. He eventually cut off the rear half of the body by hand with chisels and hammers, and thus converted it to a pickup truck!).

Usually seven or eight of us were loaded into the car for a 7:00 a.m. departure. Preparations had been made the night before with beach blankets, towels and olive oil or Vaseline for sunburn all stored in the trunk. We brought our food and drink from home: mountains of sandwiches, garden tomatoes and cucumbers, lemonade and homemade root beer, and perhaps a watermelon or grapes from the Worcester Market.

Our destination was normally York Beach, Maine. As teen-agers, Olive, Pearl and Gladys had live-in summer waitress jobs at Cobb's Restaurant there and this was an opportunity to visit them. In other years, we went to Hampton Beach, New Hampshire, less desirable in Ma's eyes because of the suspect attractions of its boardwalk, casino games and loud jazz music—or to Wells Beach, Maine.

We followed Route 140 through many cities and towns until we reached Route 1 or 1A at Salisbury. These were narrow, two-lane roads compared to the turnpikes and throughways of today. The seventy-five or eighty mile journey took about five hours depending on traffic conditions, at a maximum speed of forty-five miles an hour. There were many roadside diversions to pass the time: gas station specials—"8 gallons for a dollar"—Burma-Shave slogans to be read from several sequential signs, hot dog stands advertising "12 inches for 10 cents," the city streets of Leominster, Lowell, Lawrence, Haverhill and Merrimac, and finally the bigger-than-life wooden figure of an old salt on the barn in Salisbury—"The Old Man of the Sea." We competed for the first ocean sighting or smell of salt air as we proceeded up Route 1.

After four or five hours of dashing into the surf, building sand castles, sun-bathing and eating all available food, it was time to begin the long drive home, hoping to get back by 9:00 p.m.. One measure of the success of these outings was the "sunburn quotient." The redder you were, the better. The final criterion of a successful sunburn was to peel, not just flakes of epidermis, but long strips of semi-transparent tissue pulled carefully from shoulders or back, revealing the pink flesh underneath and calling for copious applications of olive oil or other soothing ointments. Thank goodness, melanoma hadn't been discovered yet!

The ultimate beach trips were our overnight camping junkets. These called for even more detailed logistical planning. Food supplies, cooking utensils, dishes and silverware were required. Blankets, sheets, towels and other flat goods were stacked on the car seats, giving us an elevated view of the roadside. In addition, we all brought "best" clothes to be worn at the Berwick, Maine, Methodist Church Sunday service. Somehow, we arrived at the church clean and polished and looking as if we had just emerged from our bathroom at home.

Our first encampment in an apple orchard inland from York Beach went rather well since we had brought a large Army tent, tied onto the car roof. I don't recall that we asked permission of the owner of the orchard to use it in this way. The second camp was pitched at dusk—I suppose to avoid detection—in a field inland from Hampton Beach. We did not bring the tent this time, but laid our blankets and sheets in the sweet-smelling grass. It was unbelievably pleasant to be surrounded by your family, looking up at the sky ablaze with stars, and so to fall into dreamless sleep. We were rather startled to discover in the first rays of the morning sun that we had camped in an old cemetery and were surrounded with gravestones! Several grazing cows invaded our site while we were eating breakfast. All in all, these were unforgettable moments: building our stone fireplaces, gathering wood, cooking over an open fire, singing a few old songs or hymns before bedtime.

As we journeyed through New Hampshire and Maine and down the dirt roads leading to York, Hampton or Wells Beach, we observed gypsy encampments in fields and woods. These swarthy people with long black hair sold their baskets woven of sweet-smelling grasses along the roadside. It may be that some of them were Indians. Ma and Pa stopped occasionally to buy a basket. Since we were often seeking a similar campsite, these people seemed like kindred spirits—fellow-travelers—to me.

In later years, when the tribulations of the Depression times had somewhat subsided, we spent two or three days at an old Victorian summer lodge on Wells Beach's Cobble Cove. This hotel had been for many years the Pratt family vacation destination, and they were there when we arrived. We cooked our meals with them in the common kitchen available to guests. From our vantage point on the front porch we were awed by the crashing surf as it boiled over rocks and ledges, marvelled at the moon's rays reflected from the surface of the undulating sea, and rose early to watch the sun slowly emerge on the eastern horizon, perhaps to imagine in our minds' eye the far distant shore of France. Lobstermen pulled their traps from dories just off shore. Later, we examined the strange creatures which they had caught, now on display in the lobster pound just down the road. We could never afford to buy lobsters. Rightly or wrongly, they were considered to be rich people's food.

Although on this occasion we slept in real beds, had cooking privileges in the communal kitchen, and bathrooms with running water, this sojourn as "tourists" never quite measured up to the pure elation experienced in our family camp sites.

Inspired by Arnold Pratt's passion for trains which we now shared, we drove to the Wells Railroad Station to stand on the platform as the crack Portland to Bangor nightly passenger express roared through at upwards of sixty miles an hour. We put our ears to the track to hear early ringing sounds of its approach

long before it came into sight. Then at last its powerful head-
light beams cut through the darkness as it rounded a curve, the
piercing scream of its whistle sounding ever louder. It rushed
past in a terrifying display of mechanical power, and in a moment was gone, its red observation platform lamps finally disappearing up the tracks.

My older sisters Olive, Pearl and Gladys, shortly to be
joined by Charlie and Dick, were now in their late teens or early
twenties. As is true in any generation, they associated more and
more with new-found friends who shared more sophisticated
recreational interests than these simple bucolic family pleasures.
Their jobs provided the financial independence to enjoy excursions to Boston or other destinations, bowling, golf and horse-
back riding. On a given Saturday morning they might appear
dressed in the full regalia of "riding to hounds"—highly polished
boots or jodhpurs, breeches, jackets and caps, and holding a
riding crop. So attired in the Great Gatsby tradition, they would
depart for a riding stable. They might even have been found in
attendance at polo matches sponsored by members of Worcester's "nut and bolt" aristocracy and so enjoy, at least vicariously,
one aspect of "upper crust" social life.

CHAPTER VI

New Horizons

The Barbershop

SLOWLY, BY DIMLY PERCEIVED STEPS AND EVENTS, and with inborn dread of the unknown, we become aware of the world and its people which exist beyond our home, our family and neighborhood. These first ventures are etched permanently in our memory. Certainly this was true for me on the occasion of my first visit to the barbershop. It had been decided when I reached the age of three that it was time to cut the long, blonde curls which hung half-way to my waist. I was worried that this might hurt. My brother Fred drove me to Mr. Curtis' shop at the corner of Chandler and June Street in Pa's Oldsmobile. Its shiny, chrome-plated emergency brake lever took my mind off the forthcoming shearing. Mr. Curtis was a kindly man, with a white neatly trimmed moustache, and dressed in a white jacket over his starched shirt and necktie. He quickly dispelled my concerns. I was seated on a special padded board that fit over the porcelain arms of the barber chair. From this vantage point I could see myself in the large mirror, was reassured by the reflection of Fred standing behind me, and could wonder at the long-necked silver-capped hair tonic bottles of many colors which lined the mirrored shelves. The electric shears startled me, but I braved it out and was rewarded with a dousing of witch hazel tonic followed by a scalp rub, a real "part" on the left side of my head and a red lollipop. And so, I took a first faltering step toward manhood!

School Days

Phyllis, Betty and I were the first of our family to attend the new May Street School—kindergarten through grade six—which was about a half-mile or more south of our house, beyond the old Lincoln Farm. All other kids in our family had gone to Tatnuck School through grade eight—a mile or so north of our house at the corner of Pleasant and Mill Streets. Ma walked me hand-in-hand to my first day in kindergarten. We were accompanied by sister Phyllis who, as a second-grader, was wise in the ways of schools and full of assurances which I did not really believe. These worries were shortly to be borne out. A crowd of kids my age were standing in the hallways looking unhappy; some were crying. Among the many traumatic events of that day, we were lined up by a stern-faced nurse and paraded by an even more forbidding doctor in a white coat who stuck three needles into our arms as immunization against the childhood plagues of measles, mumps, and diphtheria. Whatever he may have become in later life, I will always remember Donald Klein as the kid who threw up all over the nurse's white uniform—and the clinic floor as well!

As things settled down I found happy things as well: big wooden building blocks, my own desk, and a story hour every day! I mastered the way to the cloak room, the boys' "basement," the water bubbler, playgrounds, boys' and girls' lines in and out of the building, and the bells which signalled the beginning and end of the day's events.

Our school days began with morning devotions at home after older members of the family had left for their jobs. Ma or Pa would read a passage from the Bible—often a Psalm or other Old Testament chapter—followed by a hymn and the Lord's Prayer. We walked to and from school in all seasons, and usually home for dinner at noon as well. School was almost never canceled because of bad weather. I can't remember that this ever happened, although we listened hopefully on blizzard days for the siren signal. The plows created snow canyons higher than our heads as we trudged down the road, bundled up in wool coats, hats, mittens, scarves around our mouths, and buckled overshoes on our feet. Rainy days called for rubbers with "tongues" covering our shoelaces, and wool hats and coats. No one I knew had a real raincoat. School buses were an innovation of the far future. Mothers had neither the vehicles nor the time and inclination to drive kids back and forth when they were perfectly able to get there on their own steam. We were usually joined by other kids who lived around us. I suppose this walking would be classed as beneficial aerobic exercise today, even though we did not wear prescribed walking shoes and suits! As we retraced our steps homeward and rounded the bend in the road, it was always reassuring to catch sight of our poplar trees and behind them, the peaked turret of "552." We often took "long ways" home as well—through the Lincoln Farm fields, around the cesspool to look for frogs, turtles or snakes, then across the stone path through the swamp which led to the back fields, and finally through woodland paths to our own back yard. We picked spring wild flowers for Ma, and in the fall brought her brilliant-colored leaves. Fall was also the time we feasted on wild grapes, and "pig nuts" which littered the ground. We cracked the nuts open on the stone wall.

Boys' school clothes through grade eight were below-the-knee "knickers," long stockings held up by garters when they weren't telescoped down around your ankles, heavy-duty shoes or ankle-height sneakers, buttoned shirt, often a bow tie as well and, in fall and spring, a hand-knitted wool sweater. During the winter months we wore long underwear union suits. The legs of these stretched evermore so they were wrapped around our legs, producing a very lumpy-looking pair of calves as we pulled our stockings over them. My favorite winter garment was a hip-length black leather belted jacket with a red wool lining, topped off by my red wool toque. I wore this uniform continually until I finally grew out of it at about age eleven. Girls always wore dresses or skirts—never slacks or shorts—and long above-the-knee stockings.

The school day began with boys lined up at the boys' back door and the girls at their back door, under the watchful eye of a teacher. Shortly thereafter, we marched into our assigned rooms and to our desks. Our second set of "morning exercises" began with a Bible reading and The Lord's Prayer. We soon discovered who was Protestant or Catholic by participation or lack thereof in the final phrases—"for thine is the Kingdom . . ." Jewish kids either participated or not, as they wished, and raised no objections to this practice. Neither did Christian kids, teachers and parents object to Jewish kids being absent from school during Jewish holy days as well as those observed by Christians. Perhaps these circumstances indicated mutual respect for each others' religious beliefs. The "Salute To The Flag," and a rendition of either "My Country 'Tis of Thee," "America The Beautiful," or "The Star Spangled Banner" ended these preliminaries.

Lessons were conducted in an orderly fashion: more difficult subjects in the morning—arithmetic, reading, spelling, writing—followed in the afternoon by the more enjoyable subjects of history, geography, music, art, penmanship, and an end-of-day story reading. All classes were taught by the same teacher in the same room. We had no physical education as such, but our self-initiated playground games more than satisfied these needs. Neither was science taught in grammar school. The closest things to it were the physiographic—geologic aspects of geography. Geography was taught every year from Grade 3 through Grade 8 using the *Atwood Series* which led us eventually through the United States, Europe, Central and South America, Asia and a grand finale on New England.

The day ended with the 3:30 bell, preceded by a period of putting our desks and our room "in order." At a signal from our teacher we first sat up straight, then stood by our seats, and finally paraded by rows out the classroom door, down the halls to the front doors to await the final dismissal by our principal, Miss Barrett, together with her admonitions not to push, shove, run down the sidewalks or walk on the lawns. Disturbances in the lines could lead to a fifteen-minute stay-after-school penalty which, I must admit, was often my destiny.

Our school program included special once-a-week classes in art, music and penmanship, conducted by teachers who travelled from school to school; their specialties were reinforced daily by our regular teachers. We also received our own copy of *My Weekly Reader* for news of the day and participated in a school savings program sponsored by the Worcester Five-Cents Savings Bank. Pennies, nickels and sometimes even dimes were inserted in a cardboard folder which, when filled, was deposited in a real bank account collecting interest! We also looked forward to the annual visit of Mr. Arthur Adams, Photographer, who lined us up on the front stairs to record our progress

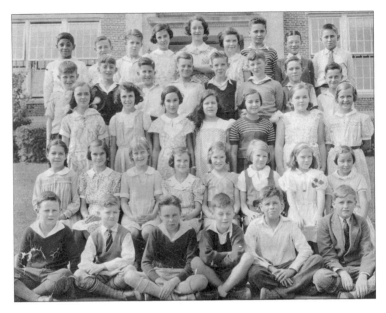

Days of Real Happiness: May Street School—Grade Six, 1934

through the grades, in pictures entitled *Days of Real Happiness.*

We made valentines at home with kits bought at Woolworth's or Kresge's and exchanged them with everyone in our class, depositing them in a box on the teacher's desk, who then appointed "mailmen" to deliver them to our desks. While this was a universal exchange between everyone—boys and girls— still I could not quite believe that my card would be delivered to Dorothy Davis, and that I would really get one from her as well. In the waning days of the higher grades of five and six, we also passed around Autograph Books in which we wrote or received some variations on "Good Luck," "Best Wishes," etc., signed, Your Friend, ...

Our classrooms were brightly decorated during the Christmas season, including our art class creations. We sang the traditional carols with no objections from civil liberty-minded zealots.

Lunch was eaten at our desks on really bad weather days—sandwiches brought from home along with a jar of milk, although some kids bought a half-pint of milk for a nickel. The school hot lunch programs of today were unknown. The most intriguing lunches were those of Nelson Dadah and his brothers and sisters. They ate with great relish many exotic foods that I had never heard of: salami and other spiced meats and cheeses between thick slices of black pumpernickel bread, little hot peppers, garlic, onions, huge apples, oranges, peaches and plums, and, wonder of wonders, pomegranates which dyed their teeth red! The fragrance of these delicacies made my mouth water. They were Syrians, I think, and their father owned Dadah's Market at the corner of Glendale and Mill Streets. These lunchtime odors blended with others of the school—sawdust and wintergreen oil compound used by the janitor in sweeping floors, damp clothes hanging in the cloak room, sour spilled milk, chalk, ink, and sweaty semi-washed bodies—creating an unforgettable olfactory impression. The essence of these "perfumes" really hasn't changed much and can still be detected in the schools of today!

A number of choice jobs assisting the teachers were vied for, even at the risk of being called a teacher's pet, because of the opportunity to escape for a time from the confines of our desk or room: empty wastebaskets, pick up lunch milk cases, fill inkwells, wash out paint brushes, or clap blackboard erasers—outside of the building! For a few cherished minutes we were free to wander through the hallways to peek through the doors of other rooms and even to descend to the boiler room where the janitor held sway. I remember our janitor better than I remember some of my teachers; I think his name was Mr. O'Connor. He reminded me of both Uncle Fred and Mr. Halpin. He smoked a pipe as they did and, like them, he did not talk much. Still it felt like I really was talking with him because of the way he was—quiet, calm, friendly. He went about his business without complaint. I liked to watch him shovel coal into the hot, raging flames of the boiler, or rake the clinkers out onto the floor to cool. The boiler room is where boys were sent to dry out if, somehow or other, they had got soaked through on the way to school or at recess. (I don't know where the girls went; maybe they never got wet!)

During each winter of my seventh, eighth and ninth years I was confined at home for most of January, February and part of March as the spring school term began. I dreaded those times during which I developed continuous wracking, hacking coughs. My maladies were considered bronchitis, whooping cough or croup, although I suspect they may have included liberal touches of pneumonia as well. I spent my days and nights on a couch-bed by the kitchen windows, warmed by the stove, where I could observe the icicles growing from the porch gutter, the winter birds feeding, and the growth and shrinkage of the snow drifts in the yard. I ate my meals here as well, and never ventured out-of-doors. My constant companions were my chamber-pot "spittoon," assorted bottles of cough syrup, and Ma's ministrations of mustard plasters and inhalings of Vick's Vap-o-Rub in steam. I was often terrified by my uncontrollable coughing spells and accompanying sweats, chills and fevers, and wondered in the wee hours of the morning, when everyone was asleep, if I was going to die. From time to time Dr. Boyden or Dr. Jewett would assess my progress. With the approach of spring, the sun rising higher and warmer each day, I often sang, at Ma's request, the old song, "When It's Springtime in the Rockies." Whatever it was, I outgrew it. Meanwhile, Phyllis brought me my school books and assignments to complete at home and so I was able to keep up with my class and rejoin my friends in time for the spring games.

Throughout the grammar school years, my favorite subjects were geography, history, reading, music and sometimes arithmetic. I usually managed to earn an "A" grade in them, with occasional lapses into a "B." Equally consistently, my least-liked subjects were grammar, spelling and penmanship, usually resulting in a "B" or "C" grade. Diagramming sentences never made much sense to me; neither did the memorization of the parts of speech and the rules governing spelling and punctuation. My concentric circles, ovals and zig-zags of the Palmer Penmanship System looked like bailing wire that had sprung loose, and were never confined between the blue lines of our penmanship paper. Large, messy blots appeared from dipping my pen too deeply in the inkwell, or from applying too much pressure to my penpoint, thereby puncturing my paper. Ma viewed with particular consternation my frequent B's in Effort, and with alarm, the C's in Conduct which were recorded all too often.

Like all kids, I relentlessly pursued the daily adventures of my favorite comic strip characters: Slim Jim, Skeezix in Gasoline Alley, Popeye and Olive Oyl, Tarzan of the Apes, Little Orphan Annie, Sandy and Daddy Warbucks. These were augmented with high-adventure books which still rank high in my lifetime reading list: *Robin Hood, Treasure Island, Robinson Crusoe, Kidnapped, Two Years Before The Mast, King Arthur and the Knights of the Round Table*, the voyages of Donald MacKay's clipper ships—*(The Flying Cloud, The Sovereign of the Seas,* et al.), *The Deerslayer, The Last of the Mohicans, The Adventures of Tom*

Sawyer, and also *The Adventures of Jimmy Mouse*—he thought the moon was made of green cheese and struggled valiantly, albeit unsuccessfully, to journey to this mouse utopia.

As with most kids then and today, some of the happiest hours were spent in the school yard during the morning recess, the noon hour, and before school. Most of the games we played were inherited from past generations of kids and in turn have been passed on in one variation or another to those who followed us.

By the time Stanley Cross (my best friend) and I, along with other classmates, had reached the fourth grade we had heard quite a repertoire of bad or naughty words from one source or another. We exchanged them and practiced "swearing" at the back of the school yard during recess until the novelty of this forbidden practice wore off.

Running games were favored in the fall: tag, red-rover, king of the mountain, football. We built snowmen, igloos and snow forts in winter. Boys built thread-spool tractors with jack-knife-notched wheels and a melted paraffin lump on one end for lubrication. These were powered by an elastic band threaded through the spool and retained at the ends by match sticks. We raced them on our desks or in the aisles until they were confiscated.

Early spring thaws made rivulets along the banks of snow beside the roadsides, carving ice shelves which we could crack all the way to school! We built slush dams in vain attempts to contain the flood, reminiscent of our summertime sand ramparts along the ocean shore, built to keep the tide from invading our castle moats. It was also the time to kick a tin can all the way to school and back, to float sailboats made of scrap lumber and a paper sail in brooks and streams hoping they might find their way to the sea—perhaps to Spain, to marvel at the tree tops stirring and swaying in gusty March winds.

Spring heralded the advent of the marbles season: "ringies," "line-ees" or "poonies" for boys, "bunny-in-the-hole" for girls. My collection often reached twenty-five or even fifty marbles, including the prized "glassies" and "aggies" of many sizes. On several occasions, while I was sitting at my desk, the bulging pockets of my knickers burst under the strain, cascading these treasures onto the floor in all directions only to have them commandeered by my teacher until after school, thus putting me out of the competition for the rest of the day. From these experiences I learned to keep my marbles in a cloth sugar or salt bag.

Girls also played hop-scotch, jacks, and several varieties of jump-rope while the boys on their side of the playground spun tops and yo-yo's, gambled with baseball or Indian tribe cards by scaling them against a wall, or played baseball catch—no bats allowed on the playground. Boys whacked at each others' "horse-cobbler" nuts suspended by a shoelace, often rapping our competitor's knuckles in the process. These cobblers (horse chestnuts) had been painstakingly baked in our mothers' ovens to an optimum hardness and were rated by how many weaker ones had been broken—"mine's a 'niney,'" or a "seventeener."

I, along with other boys of eleven or twelve years, developed a rather feisty, contentious spirit in general, and in particular in regards to the outcome of our playground contests. Fist fights, wrestling or a combination of both often erupted during recess, although, by mutual consent, these battles were usually deferred until "after school—behind the school." By dismissal time, the rumor mill had done its job, resulting in a crowd gathered to watch the forthcoming fisticuffs. The observers egged both contestants on, who then were honor-bound to fight even though tempers might have cooled by then, and despite the lead-weight-sinking feeling in the pit of one's stomach. Things began slowly, more exchanges of words and threats, followed by tentative exchanges of shoves, and finally to punches, pulling on arms and roly-poly wrestling, with the cheers and shouts of the audience sounding strangely far away. A bloody nose or cut lip or two, swollen ears or eyes, and ripped shirts or pants usually ended the contest with no clear victor emerging. We just got too tired to continue.

The sequels to these battles were worse than the events themselves. On the one hand, if these fights occurred during the school day, Miss Barrett, our principal, was sure to have learned of it one way or another. The result was at least a week of one-hour after school sessions in her office, during which we wrote 500 times in ink, "I must not fight in the school yard" and were required to bring a note home to be signed by our parents. By the end of these confinements, former enemies often became friends out of mutual sympathy. I confess at this late date to a Pyrrhic Victory—I only wrote 487 sentences instead of the pre-scribed 500!

On the other hand, whether the fight occurred during or after school, Ma was sure to know about it via Miss Barrett's note, a neighborhood tattletale, or simply on the evidence of my ripped clothes, bruises and abrasions. I was then required, despite this double jeopardy, to cut a "sturdy birch switch" to be applied liberally to my legs as I performed a gandy-dancers jig to avoid the same; and I was not allowed out of the house after supper. One of my debates with myself as I plodded to the woods to cut my own switch was, "What is the smallest, weakness, thinnest one I can get away with?"

The Lincoln Farm fields (later to become the Normal School/State College playing fields), were our after-school base-ball diamond and football gridiron despite the grass which often stood a foot or more in height. We picked up sides—for baseball by the time-honored fist-over-fist-on-the-bat by the two captains of the day to decide who got "first pick" of players—for football by the old odd or even fingers ploy. It was infinitely better to be a "picker" rather than a "pick-ee," since the latter suffered the pains of waiting to be picked, and the possibility that you might end up being the last pick and thereby consigned to play right field, with admonitions not to drop any flies, and not to strike out, either! Our tackle football, without protective equipment of any kind, was a rough and tumble affair resulting in more ripped clothes and bloody noses to be explained at home and bearing little resemblance to the sophisticated little league contests of today.

We also played war on the hillsides behind stone wall trenches, using pieces of sod or dirt clods as hand grenades or bombs. Arguments as to whether we were dead or just wounded by these missiles were seldom resolved amicably. We took turns being Americans or Germans. I wore Fred's steel helmet, leggings and gas mask which he brought home from his Army service, and thus often got elected captain by virtue of my superior equipment!

Walking Tours

I had several alternate walking routes to Saturday morning choir practice at the church, all of which provided a variety of interesting sights and activities. By cutting through Halpins' field to May Street and thence down Pleasant Street to Newton Square, I might catch a glimpse of frogs, toads, turtles, or a black snake along the brook, and pick an apple or two in the old orchard trees before proceeding along the hilly sections of these streets. Boys not much older than I could be observed "hooking" free rides on the back steps or bumper of the Pleasant Street trolley cars. I decided to learn this skill. On other days I made my way down Chandler Street to June Street, pausing briefly at the candy store before heading for Newton Square. (For a nickel I could get refueled with a Mars Bar, Milky Way or Three Musketeers. A dime bought a box of Cracker-Jacks, with a free toy inside. My favorite toys were those "clickers" painted like a beetle. You could put them under your shoe in school and click them without detection until some teacher's pet stared at your foot long enough for the teacher to discover who was creating the disturbance. The confiscation of my clicker and another fifteen-minute after-school punishment could be expected.)

At the Newton Square junction, I observed tennis matches in progress on the public courts before continuing on down Highland Street. Sometimes I detoured over Newton Hill with its woods and cliffs, and crossed Park Avenue to Elm Park, with its flocks of ducks and geese feeding in its ponds. If I continued down Pleasant Street I would pass Blessed Sacrament Church. Still further along this route I examined the new cars in the show windows of Park Avenue automobile dealers. I finally headed for our church through a maze of residential streets lined with imposing homes of wealthy burghers.

Blessed Sacrament held a special fascination for me, inspired by my inquisitiveness about the unknown. The massive front doors of this gothic edifice were frequently open, revealing the high altar at the far end of the dimly lit interior. The altar was partially illuminated by flickering flames from banks of candles in little red glass cups on either side; a larger-than-life crucifix hung above it. Long lines of statues could be made out in the gloom of the side aisles. Except for all the statues and candles, this sanctuary looked quite a bit like that of my Wesley Methodist Church; it even had a rose window similar to ours. Priests in flowing medieval robes and capes scurried back and forth as they performed their mysterious rites. Sometimes they appeared on the front steps, and even waved a greeting to me. I often met school-mates there on their way to confession and altar boy practice, whatever these activities were. Perhaps the priests thought I was another one of their charges. Although consumed with curiosity, I resisted the urge to step inside for a closer look. It was rumored among us Protestants that Catholics, especially priests, would try to convert you and thereby earn another star in their crown—seven stars would guarantee them entrance into heaven while avoiding both purgatory and hell. Conversely, it was rumored among some Catholic kids that Protestants, especially ministers, might try to steal their soul and sell it to the devil. For these reasons we never ventured into each other's churches no matter how friendly we might be in the schoolyard or during athletic contests.

New York City

One of the most memorable events of my eleventh year was a three-day trip to New York City with Mr. Jacobs, our church organist and choir director. He and Mrs. Jacobs, who was also a church musician, had rewarded three of us who were children's choir members in this way based on our attendance, knowledge of our music, and, I suppose, other criteria. My sister Olive bought me a three-piece Harris Tweed knicker suit and a matching felt hat to boot for this occasion. Louise Mohler, whom I secretly liked, and Barbara Chaffee were the other two lucky kids. We traveled to New York in the Jacobs' 1933 Ford sedan via the Merritt Parkway, and slept and ate in the Algonquin Hotel, near Times Square. This gave us easy access to the fabled square as well as to Radio City Music Hall and a Rockettes' stage show. We strolled Park Avenue and Fifth Avenue, ate in the Automat and rode the subways and double-decker buses to the Cathedral of St. John the Divine. There we heard the boy's choir and toured their choirboy school facilities. While there I sang Gounod's "Sanctus" in Latin, one of my church solo numbers. I often wondered if Mr. Jacobs had presented me there as a candidate but I never heard any more about it. I shall always be grateful to the Jacobses for this experience.

My Bike

Pa bought me a red, second-hand one-speed bicycle for my twelfth birthday. This greatly increased my mobility, excluding flat tire time, as I journeyed the three miles several times a week to church for choir rehearsal, Boy Scout meetings, Sunday school and piano lessons, to athletic contests, and around my paper route. This also made it easy for me to attend the home football games of Worcester Polytechnic Institute. Pa was groundskeeper there and I got in free, usually sitting just behind the team on the 50-yard line. I was there when the storied Jackie Germain lofted his 90-yard down-wind punt! Pa and I joined the coaches and officials in the field house at half-time for sandwiches and coffee. The bike also allowed me to explore Main Street on my own. Here I browsed through the sporting goods stores, admiring the tents, camping equipment, toboggans, skis, snowshoes, baseball gloves and bicycles. I gawked at the lurid announcements posted at Mechanics Hall for current or forthcoming boxing and wrestling matches, roller-skating tournaments and marathon dances, and further on, the theater advertisements for movies featuring Hedy Lamarr in *Ecstasy* and similar verboten shows. A White Tower ten-cent hamburger "smothered in onions" and a half pint of McCann's three-flavored ice cream for a nickel staved off my hunger pangs until supper time.

Tatnuck School

My school days of real happiness ended when I graduated from the sixth grade at May Street and transferred to Tatnuck School to complete the last two years of grammar school. I had done pretty well in academic subjects and so our principal, Miss Barrett, recommended that I be enrolled in Sever Street Prep. This program included French, German and Latin as well as "mathematics," rather than arithmetic, and was intended for students who eventually would go on to college. However, in my mind the traditions and honor of the Kemp family were at stake here. All the children of our family, except Phyllis, Betty and I were Tatnuck-educated. Charlie had a well-deserved reputation as the best short stop and homerun hitter the school had seen in many years; I wanted to follow in his footsteps. Fred had an unblemished and unchallenged record as the best school-boy boxer-wrestler ever seen in these parts. I also wanted to reach this high standard of combative skill. Besides, I had no idea what "college" was, and if asked, could not have told you if it was spelled with one "l" and two "g's" or vice versa. I persuaded Ma to let me go to Tatnuck where things did not turn out quite as I had hoped. All of my true friends went on to other schools. I became the new boy on the block; a "pick-ee" for athletics rather than a "pick-er."

I quickly found out that there were several boys tougher than I was, among them Howard Cooper who was a disciplinary terror for teachers in the classroom, and who struck fear in the hearts of many kids on the playground as well. I responded to his challenge to box "bare knuckles." He had a rapid-fire jab which made jelly of my nose and closed both of my eyes. On the other hand, I was stronger and was able to continually pin him at wrestling. I suppose we ended in a draw and thus developed a sort of mutual respect for each other. Howard was also from a very large family of ten or twelve kids where he was at the same level on the totem pole as I was. He had his family traditions to uphold as well.

The field of combat for these contests was just across Chandler Street from Drolet's Garage and Good Gulf Gasoline Station. They conducted their business from their barn which had formerly been a horseshoeing and blacksmithing establishment. The old forge and anvils were still in place, and other tools of these trades still hung on the walls. Creamers', next door to the field, sold ice cream from their enclosed front porch, with the selection limited to vanilla, chocolate or strawberry. However, I often "licked my wounds" while licking a five-cent cone from Creamers' before heading homewards.

Manual Training

All boys in Grades 7 and 8 at Tatnuck School took an afternoon weekly class in "manual training," while the girls learned to cook and sew in "domestic arts" classes. These lessons were conducted at Oxford Street School, near the center of the city. We boys all made identical products with hand-powered tools—a mahogany footstool, a pine bookcase, and a pirate ship complete with hand-tied rigging, rat-lines, and sails cut from thin copper sheeting, with the finished model painted in black, gold and shellac. Our instructor was Mr. Holmquist, my first male teacher. He presided over the ranks of individual work benches from his stool behind an imposing work bench of his own.

Our first class was held in the third week of the fall. I had just entered Tatnuck and found this new prospect very intriguing. However, my optimism was short-lived. Things just got off to a bad start. Mr. Holmquist, in his introductory remarks, told us that we were free to walk about the shop to get tools, compare techniques or to come to his bench for help. This sounded just great after having been confined to a desk for six grades. He also said we could whisper and chat with each other. This was my downfall; I thought he said we could *whistle*. I was quite proud of my skill in this musical medium, usually whistling old-time tunes all the way around my paper route or most any other place out-of-doors. To demonstrate my whistling ability, I let go with a piercing note, followed by the first few bars of "Red River Valley." I was stopped in mid-note by Mr. Holmquist who bellowed, "Oh, a wise-guy in the class already. I know how to take care of trouble makers. Kemp, get out of my shop now, and don't come back until you have a note from your principal and your parents asking me to take you back—and a letter of apology from you as well!" My attempts to explain that I thought he said "whistle" instead of "whisper" were to no avail as he held the door open for my hasty exit.

There I was, stranded three miles from home with a light rain falling, and not a nickel to my name for car fare. We had come as a class on the Pleasant Street trolley, with one-way tickets provided at Tatnuck, the return ticket to be provided by Mr. Holmquist. Needless to say, he declined to give me one. It was a long, lonely walk back to Tatnuck. On the way I tried to sort

things out. How had this happened? True, I tended to be en-
thusiastic, maybe a little exuberant or boisterous at times when I
was excited about something. Ma said from time to time that I
acted as if I had "St. Vitus' Dance" (an affliction of hyper-active
children). Be that as it may, I had never thought of myself as a
wise-guy or a trouble-maker. This was a fine kettle of fish—only
at Tatnuck for three weeks and already in deep trouble. How was
I going to explain this disastrous development to Ma and Pa? I
decided to face the music with Miss Cunningham, our principal,
first, although I had never met her. Even with quite a bit of foot-
dragging, I arrived at her office before three o'clock. It was almost four o'clock before she could see me. Now I was in even
more trouble. I was already a half-hour late for my paper route,
and would probably be late for supper as well.

I did get my three notes with which I was re-admitted to
manual training. However, my reputation with Mr. Holmquist
remained tarnished despite my best efforts to be a model of
decorum. I ended up with a "C" grade. I really did enjoy making
the footstool and gave it to Ma for Christmas. My pirate ship
graced the bookcase in my room for several years. It disappeared
during my three years in the Navy, probably a casualty of a super
spring cleaning spree.

Logan Field, with its real baseball diamond and backstop,
officially lined football field with goal posts, its tennis and basketball courts, became a vast improvement over the Lincoln
Farm hayfields of yore. I spent many hours there with the Tatnuck Square gang. Kenny O'Donnell always captained our pick-
up teams for baseball, football and basketball, the latter being a
game I previously had never heard of. His father was head football coach at Holy Cross College and had taught him the real

basics as well as the use of plays and strategy.

We challenged neighborhood football teams from Newton Square, Abbott Field and even Webster Square. We had no coaches or recreation directors to arrange these matches. We did it on our own through the word-of-mouth, rumor-mill network used by all boys then and I suppose even these days. No referees mediated disputes. These were settled by yelling matches, trade-off compromises, or by the flip of a coin. No penalties were called since there was no one to call them. Games were played non-stop for about an hour and a half by someone's watch. We did not observe the niceties of quarter-time and half-time breaks.

Our parents were largely unaware of these contests. They had enough to do without getting involved in our fun and games. Besides, we would have been inhibited, uncomfortable or embarrassed to have them in attendance. Certainly, we never expected them to provide transportation. We got to the playing fields in the same way we got anywhere—walking, biking or "hooking" rides on the back of trolley cars.

Although our football field was "regulation," our equipment was not. We played tackle without protective equipment. Our uniforms were old pants, sweaters and our ordinary high-top sneakers. I did own a discarded leather helmet from W.P.I. which fit so tightly that it gave me headaches after a few plays. However, it helped me earn the right to play the hard-charging center and sometimes right tackle. Billy Gibbs, at right end, occasionally wore shoulder pads, borrowed from his brother who was a member of the Classical High School team. Similarly, Kenny O'Donnell, at quarterback, wore his brother's helmet from time to time, although he preferred to play bare-headed, as did we all.

For me, our most memorable gridiron battle was played against the Abbott Field gang at Logan Field in the fall of 1936. They were considered to be unbeatable largely because of their fullback, a 170-pound monster almost six feet tall who wore heavy, size 12 clod-hopper boots. He was known to us as "The Goon." I never knew his real name. He never uttered a word; we wondered if he could talk. He scored all of their touchdowns simply by plowing right through center, stomping and trampling under foot anyone who got in his way. Since we were all just a few inches over five feet tall at best, and weighed somewhere between 90 and 100 pounds, he was a formidable opponent. The only way we could bring him down to earth was to have five or six of us climb on his back or hang onto his arms and legs, and ultimately to trip him until he fell to earth with a thump and a groan. As the game progressed he took on the image of a Frankenstein apparition with a pack of wildcats clinging to his frame.

By sheer grit and stubbornness, we stayed in the game, goal for goal. While they played an exclusively running offense, we matched it with our pass and run game. Time after time, Kenny's bullet passes found fleet-footed Billy Gibbs at right end, or half-back Marty Wilson around left end. Finally, the score stood at 24 to 24 with only two minutes to play. They had the ball on our fifteen yard line with four downs to go. At their center's snap of the ball, the cry went out from us all—"Here comes The Goon through center!" He did, gathering momentum as he crossed the scrimmage line. I was at right tackle. As he mowed down our line and backfield, I made a desperate flying tackle at those feet shod in lethal boots. Wonder of wonders, he dropped like a ton of bricks as my arms encircled his ankles in a death grip. I remember the heel of his boot as it struck my mouth, and the ball squirting out from under him as he fell. Before I passed out, I remember thinking that I was somehow like David bringing down Goliath—with his sling shot! Some Tatnuck-eer, probably Marty Wilson, scooped the ball up, and with a spectacular display of broken-field running, ran through the disbelieving Abbott Fielders for the final touchdown. We had won! 30 to 24!

My team-mates decided that I was too groggy to ride my bike back home. I really wasn't in the best of shape, with a bloody upper lip swollen to the size of an egg, and my left front tooth bent inward at a forty-five degree angle. Someone—it may have been Marty—was designated to walk me home pushing my bike, to explain to my mother how I got the "fat lip."

I was rushed to Dr. Bollinger, our new dentist. He drilled a hole in the back of the tooth, extracted the nerve which had been broken, and held up this quivering pink exhibit for my inspection. He then inserted a gold peg of the same shape and pushed my tooth back into its original position, supporting it with some wires. Thus, I received my first root canal. He must have been a real "pro." The tooth is still sound after fifty-five years although it has taken on a blue-grey tone with advancing years. Norman Erickson, one of my oldest friends, took to calling me "Old Blue-Tooth," which I consider to be sort of an honorary title.

I tried out valiantly for short-stop on the baseball team and the honor of wearing a real uniform with Tatnuck School emblazoned across my chest, but got cut from the squad after bobbling several hot grounders, and fanning the air at the plate while trying for the left field wall.

All was not lost, however. Tatnuck had a branch library where I could take out up to six books, even on weekends, including some of my favorite high-adventure explorer stories. It was through some of those that I became acquainted with two of my boyhood heroes: Admiral Richard E. Byrd, who explored the Antarctic regions, and Sir Malcolm Campbell of Scotland who for many years held the world's speed records on land and sea, in his Bluebird racing car on the Bonneville Salt Flats of Utah, and in his Bluebird speedboat in the off-shore waters of Daytona Beach, Florida.

Life went on. I graduated from the eighth grade at Tatnuck, even made one of the graduation speeches and got my first pair of long pants—the traditional rite of passage upon finishing grammar school. I suffered the embarrassments of voice changes from boy soprano to croaking pre-adolescent, observed my nose growing daily in Pinocchio-like stages and my face becoming a pimple-field under the influence of galloping hormones, and went off—ready or not—to the new world of high school.

Earning Money

My first lessons in the financial realities of life, beginning at about age nine, were learned at our road-side vegetable and fruit stand. I kept it under surveillance along with other members of the family as we went about other activities in the house or yard. Our products included corn, tomatoes, cucumbers, string beans, peas and summer squash from our garden; blueberries, blackberries, strawberries, raspberries and grapes picked "in the wild," apples picked at local orchards; and potatoes, carrots, beets and winter squash bought at wholesale. I learned how to talk with strangers, to display our wares to best advantage, to resist attempts to lower our prices, and to somehow discourage undue picking over of our merchandise, especially the stripping down of many ears of corn to find the best six, making the others unsalable. We recycled old grocery bags, weighed out vegetables on our scale, made change, and thanked customers for their business. On a good day we might realize two or three dollars! All revenue went into the family coffers; it never occurred to us to think otherwise. I suppose this practice made us all really contributing members of the family. From this common kitty, nickels were made available for Sunday School collections, rainy-day bus or trolley fares, weekly additions to our school savings program and perhaps an occasional ice cream cone, bag of marbles or baseball card.

My brothers Charlie and Dick had worked for Mr. Halpin, caretaker of Dr. Alton's May Street estate, mowing lawns and shovelling the long driveway and sidewalks in winter. I inherited these jobs when I was eleven or twelve years old as my brothers went on to better jobs. I earned fifty cents on Saturday mornings from 8:00 a.m. to noon. The day began by helping Mr. Halpin sharpen and oil the hand-pushed reel lawn mowers. He reminded me of Uncle Fred; he was a practical, modest, taciturn man who smoked a pipe. The Alton children and their friends, all of whom were about my age—give or take a year or two—watched from the sidelines as we mowed their croquet lawn and rolled their clay tennis court. They were nattily attired in white athletic costumes; maids served them ice-cold lemonade as their games progressed, while Mr. Halpin and I quenched our thirst from the garden hose. Except for these circumstances, our paths never crossed. I presume they attended private schools since I had never seen them at May Street School. I never did know their names, and am certain they did not know mine. Despite the vague resentments I felt toward them—especially for not sharing their lemonade—I was rather proud to be doing this work, in a Tom Sawyer-ish way. This experience, and the yard work skills learned at home were put to further use "working for wages" at other homes in the area, mowing lawns in the spring and summer, raking leaves in the fall, shovelling walks and driveways in the winter.

My next step up the ladder of economic success and independence at age twelve was the purchase of a *Worcester Evening Post* newspaper route of thirty-five customers, bought for three dollars from Norman Blodgett. The route was about four miles in length, starting at the drop-off point at Taft's Market on Pleasant Street. By learning the techniques of folding newspapers into a square or tube which could be scaled onto the porches on the run, I could cover the whole route in less than an hour, ending up at Logan Field in time for an hour or so of baseball or football. I learned how to keep a ledger, roll coins, add or drop customers and pay the collector. If all my customers paid their bills—some did not—I could make about two dollars a week, supplemented by several ten-cent tips at Christmas!

These enterprises gave me the wherewithall to begin weekly piano lessons at twenty-five cents for a half hour, to pay my Boy Scout dues and to buy uniforms and camping equipment at the Army Surplus Store, and to build up my school savings account. I felt very proud to be handling some of my own expenses with money I had earned.

Boy Scouts

I joined Troop 8, Boy Scouts of America, in my twelfth year—the entry age at that time. My troop was sponsored by our church, Wesley Methodist Episcopal. The four scouting years that followed gave me some of the most pleasurable experiences of my youth. A kaleidoscope of bright images comes to mind as

I recall those glorious days. It all started with the visit of Jimmy Spellman with Ma and me to describe the benefits of Scouting and the great times which awaited. (Jimmy was a dedicated, dynamic and hearty Boy Scout executive as well as being a friend of our family.)

Our Friday evening troop meetings were held in a magnificent panelled beamed, cathedral-ceilinged church hall. This setting brought to my mind tales of medieval knights clad in armor and gathered around great blazing fires—surrounded by their squires, pages, minstrels and beautiful maidens—as they extolled their glorious exploits in do-or-die contests with fire-breathing dragons, black-hearted lords, and countless other evil powers, in their search for the Holy Grail. Here were assembled forty or more uniformed scouts by patrols—with flags flying—as we came to attention for inspection by our several leaders: Mr. Roscoe "Pop" Blunt, Scoutmaster, and Mr. "Spence" Spencer, Assistant Scoutmaster; Mr. Munson and several other uniformed members of our troop board; our Junior Assistant Scoutmasters, Jimmy Irvine, Winnie Munson, Delbert Betterley, and Dan Webster, our Senior Patrol Leader and the consummate Boy Scout. These men exemplified to us—callow youths that we were—what it meant to be a man.

This hall was the scene of countless instructional demonstrations conducted by our leaders: packing your gear, making your own equipment, compass and map reading, outdoor cooking, first aid, Morse code, semaphore and other signal drills. Older scouts confirmed these skills with younger scouts in our patrol meetings. I still recall with pride the evening I was appointed Hawk Patrol Leader—at age fourteen—and my efforts in transmitting scouting lore to my Tenderfeet and Second-Class charges.

There was also time for fun and frolics in our game period just preceding our closing ceremonies; "Steal the Bacon" was the hands-down favorite contest.

Our troop meetings came to a close with a final assembly by patrols. Fifty or more voices fervently proclaimed once again those eternal verities summarized in the Scout Oath, the Scout Laws and the Scout Motto—to be prepared. At the command, "Troop Dismissed," fifty pairs of feet shook the very foundations of the hall. My after-dark solo journey home at "Scouts' pace"— three miles in twenty-five minutes—was a time to ponder the meaning of these experiences.

One of our most memorable troop projects was that of each scout making his own one-man tent of cheesecloth dyed forest green and soaked in melted paraffin for waterproofing; mixed with borax as a fire-retardant. Our tents did shed water but we never dared to test the fire-retardant qualities of the borax!

Most of all, I remember Treasure Valley, our regional Boy Scout summer camp. I had saved $5.00 for a week at camp; Pa gave me $5.00 for a second week! I shall never forget setting up our troop encampment: four-man tents, our canvas cots, building fireplaces, digging latrines, chopping firewood. We cooked our own breakfast and lunch, and ate dinner in the camp-wide mess tents. Together with my scouting buddies of those days— Everett and Ernest Titus, George Jordan, John Barrett, Franny Carruthers, Aram Avasian—I climbed the signal towers, built lashed bridges over brooks, raced in war-canoes, competed in scouting skill contests. We sang our hearts out around the Treasure Valley campfires—led by the raucous, boisterous, voice of Jimmy Spellman. Who could ever forget his inspired leadership as several hundred scouts bellowed "Bravo Bravissimo," or the Treasure Valley "alma mater"!

Above all, scouting taught me to be self-reliant and confident at an early age, and to try to have the courage to stand up for what I believed. It gave me an honorable code to live by. I still from time to time repeat to myself these pledges: On my honor, I will do my best, to do my duty to God and my country; to obey the Scout Laws; to help other people at all times; to keep myself physically strong, mentally awake and morally straight; to do a good turn daily; a scout is trustworthy, loyal, helpful, friendly, courteous, kind, obedient, cheerful, thrifty, brave, clean and reverent.

These precepts have had a more powerful and lasting impact on me as I try to live a good life within the limits of my human frailties than those of churches, schools, colleges, the Navy or any other organizations to which I have belonged. More than any other, they reinforced and crystallized the guideposts given to me by my parents.

I passed then, without awareness, out of the age of innocence, of simplicity; away from the secure havens of home and family—our yards, fields and woods, my school and church— and into a larger world where new, exciting, threatening things awaited; places where people and events unknown in earlier times would influence the course of my life. As these new images gained strength they seemed better—more pleasurable— than the old ways. And yet, I often return in memory and with painful nostalgia to those childhood years. Why is this? From whence comes this too-late longing for things which earlier seemed to give us contentment?

It may be that these priceless treasures—this ethereal essence of family feelings of joy, of love—never existed at all except in the wishful-thinking mind of a child. I think not. I prefer to think that this is really how things were; that for some brief moments long ago there really was something closely akin to a Kemp Camelot.

All in all, it has been, and continues to be, a good life; and I would not exchange it. I wish for those who walk with me on this "Long Long Trail," and for those who follow, the same joys that have been mine.

•

And so, Ma and Pa
for a' that, and a' that
and
a' that, and a' that;
you were better persons than I am
for a' that, and a' that.

Your Son,
James Malcolm

EPILOGUE

Preceded by the death of John, and beginning with Eva in 1923 and Fred in 1934—later accelerated by the events of World War II—the children, now adults, departed from "552" one by one to pursue their own fortunes. Olive joined the American Red Cross overseas, Pearl, Gladys, Phyllis and Betty married, as did Charlie, Dick and I during or following our military service—Charlie in the Marines, Dick and I in the Navy.

To me, the greatest tragedy which befell Ma and Pa was the sale of "552" in 1955—the home to which they had been bonded for over fifty years. It had become a monument to their lives together and was overflowing with remembrances of their children. Life was never the same for them thereafter. Restless moves from one apartment after another followed, but their wellsprings of true serenity had been hopelessly lost. Far better that they had remained in their own true home as it slowly disintegrated around them and with them.

Reunions of brothers and sisters with their spouses and offspring were held infrequently and took on the tone of ritualized pro forma gatherings at funerals or weddings, and sporadic Fourth-of-July or Christmas celebrations, with some unable to attend. Our children, as when we were children, do not know their cousins, aunts and uncles other than as superficial acquaintances, or as vague branches on the family tree.

Charlie and Dick got together off and on for a round of golf and Charlie and I for an annual day on the ski slopes. The sisters gathered by themselves more frequently in each other's homes, or in Boston-area restaurants for lunch or dinner.

The fabric which had once knit us together so closely became loosened, unbound, broken—strand by strand. Our knowledge of each other—who we now are, what we think—is limited to what we were as children rather than of what we have become. We no longer know or understand each other, share deep thoughts, express our hopes, our fears, our aspirations. We have become strangers. This is a sad turn of events when we consider that all of us will be gone from this world in a decade—two at the most—following those who have already died.

Perhaps this evolution demonstrates a struggle to escape from the frugality of our childhood, to deny or forget our humble heritage. Did we avoid each other because we served as reminders of those early days? Why this desire to become something we were not? We were worthy wardens of our world as we were.

ABOUT THE AUTHOR

James Kemp and his wife, Lavina, live in Bath, Maine—the City of Ships—on the Kennebec River. Their four adult children are widely dispersed to Massachusetts, Washington State, Nebraska and Scotland.

He retired in 1987 from East Stroudsburg University, Pennsylvania, where he served as Vice President for Academic Affairs and from time to time was acting president during periods of extended absence of the President. His previous positions include Dean for Undergraduate Studies at Boston State College where he was concurrently the originator and director of the management degree program, Director (Dean) of Continuing Education and Associate Professor at Springfield College, Personnel Manager for College Relations and Management Development with Monsanto Company's Plastics Division. As an oceanographer and marine geologist at Woods Hole Oceanographic Institution during 1951 and 1952, he participated in a major study of the North Atlantic Gulf Stream and several other scientific surveys. His career also includes appointments as a teacher, coach, and principal in the school systems of Granby and Templeton, Massachusetts. During World War II he served for three years in the United States Navy aboard warships in the Atlantic, Caribbean and Pacific Theaters.

In his high school, college and early teaching years he worked at a wide variety of jobs—short-order cook, grocery truck driver, tree cutter, an eighty-hour week machine-tool factory worker, resident estate hand, janitor, night watchman, freight-train baggage handler, and construction laborer.

Following his graduation from Classical High School in Worcester, Massachusetts, the city of his birth, he earned B.A. and M.A. degrees from Clark University and the Ed.D. degree from the University of Massachusetts. He also completed graduate study courses at Harvard University, the University of Chicago, Springfield College and the University of Maine. All of his academic degrees were completed while working full time.

He has been an adjunct professor of management and organizational psychology at both graduate and undergraduate levels with Suffolk University, Worcester Polytechnic Institute, Bunker Hill Community College, New Hampshire College and the University of Maine, and has been a management consultant and trainer with a wide variety of business, industrial, governmental and educational organizations.

Throughout his career he complemented his professional life with an active involvement in community organizations. Currently, he is a corporator and tour guide at the Maine Maritime Museum, on the Advisory Board of the Bath Chocolate Church Center for the Arts, and serves on the Long-Range Planning Committee of the Episcopal Diocese of Maine. He is a contributor to the Nature Conservancy and several other environmental protection organizations.

Previous community service efforts include elective and appointive posts with libraries and museums, adult education, industrial development, United Fund, school committees, personnel and appeals boards, Boy Scouts of America, as a P.T.A. president, Sunday school teacher and superintendent, and lay reader.

Jim is a self-taught sculptor in wood and stone, specializing in the cetaceans—whales and dolphins—and has exhibited his works in faculty art shows at East Stroudsburg University and Boston State College. He enjoys landscaping, gardening and stone-wall building, dabbles in pencil sketching and architecture, and plays the piano for his own amusement. At last count he has, through the years, sung in twenty-five different choruses, choirs and glee clubs.

He and his wife, Lavina, are lifetime skiers—both alpine and nordic. They can also be found canoeing the rivers, lakes and bays of mid-coast Maine, on occasion hoisting a sail on their canoe or iceboat to experience life on the edge of disaster, and they frequently walk the beaches and headlands of this area.

In years past, Jim was a wilderness camper and mountain climber in the White Mountains of New Hampshire—particularly in the

Presidential Range region. For over a decade in the early 1950's to early 1960's, he made an annual hiking and camping trek to Mount Washington's Tuckerman's Ravine to ski on the Headwall, Hillman's Highway and the summit snow fields in the days when only 20 to 30 people might be found on these awesome slopes. He continues to make valiant efforts to play golf and tennis with consistently poor results, but still delights in pouring his MGB sports car over the byways of the countryside.

His reading preferences are oriented toward non-fiction treatises in history, life sciences, philosophy, mythology, and religion. All in all, he has tried to pursue a Renaissance-man life style even before he knew what this term meant, insofar as his energies and abilities would allow. His favorite bumper sticker reads: *Just Do It!*